Seize the Word and Hold on No Matter What

An introduction to studying and applying the message of the Bible using a variety of popular translations, study methods, and devotional books

Paul Durbin

Dedicated to my dad, Cecil Durbin.

Your faith in Jesus, your wonder at God's creation, your gratitude for God's Grace, your hunger for the Bible, and your faithful generosity to God's people have inspired and fueled my own faith since I was a boy.

May this book inspire that same faith, wonder, gratitude, hunger, and generosity in others.

But the seed in the good earth—these are the good-hearts who seize the Word and hold on no matter what, sticking with it until there's a harvest.
Jesus, Luke 8:15 (The Message)

CONTENTS

INTRODUCTION

O ne of my favorite Bible stories is found in Luke 8. This parable of Jesus goes by a few different names (depending on the Bible version), such as *The Story of the Seeds,* or *The Parable of the Sower,* but the plot remains the same: a farmer goes out to his field to sow some seed. A few of these seeds fall on the path, others on rocky ground, some amongst thorns, and a few on good soil.

I like the way The Message tells us what becomes of the seeds that fall on the *good* soil. Luke 8:15 in that version of the Bible says, "But the seed in the good earth—these are the good-hearts who *seize the Word and hold on no matter what,* sticking with it until there's a harvest."

The difference is clear. People who choose to *seize the Word (God's Word) and hold on no matter what* are the same people who continue to move forward and bear fruit in their walk with Jesus.

Is that what you want? Do you want to keep moving *farther up and farther in* in your walk with God? ("Farther up and farther in" is a quote from C.S. Lewis's, The Last Battle—a worthwhile read).

If so, then this book was made for you. Here's how it works: this book is separated into 24 sections. Each of these sections has three parts: 1) a chapter from the book of Luke, 2) a Bible study method, and 3) a devotional reading.

1. A Chapter From The Book Of Luke

Why the book of Luke? Good question. In putting this resource together, I knew I wanted to choose one of the Gospels (because meditating on the life and words of Jesus is always a good thing). And I love the way Luke ends the story I talked about above with, *"seize the Word and hold on no matter what"* (Luke 8:15, MSG).

In truth, we really could have used any book of the Bible, because I pray that the practices you'll develop by going through this book will catapult you into a daily habit of reading the *entire* Bible (not just Luke). I put an additional section at the back of this book, *Pastor Paul's Ribbon-Tally Method for Reading the Bible,* to help you do just that.

You're also going to notice that we will not stick with just one translation of the Bible. In fact, we're going to be using *eight* different translations. Why? You'll find the answer to that in the next section of this book, *"Which Bible Translation is Best?"*

2. A Bible Study Method

I'm going to introduce you to seven different Bible study methods: S.O.A.P., R.E.A.P., 4R's, C.O.R.E, Discovery, C.U.B.E., and Manuscript. Don't worry if you don't know what any of that means just yet—I'll explain each one as they come up.

I introduce you to several different methods, because we all have our different styles of learning and making things *stick*. It's my hope that at least *one* of these methods of studying the truths of the Bible will click with you, and enable you to develop a habit of not only reading the Bible, but also applying it to your life.

3. A Devotional Reading

For generations, Jesus-Followers have felt the need to hear someone else's take on a certain scripture. To fill this need, a special kind of book—a **Christian** *devotional*—was written to help people reflect on the scripture.

A devotional is like having godly mentor sitting beside you as you read the Bible. They point out a few things of interest along the way and urge to you apply a truth (or truths) that you may have otherwise missed.

I've tried to include a few classics, such as <u>My Utmost for His Highest</u> by Oswald Chambers, <u>Morning and Evening</u> by Charles Spurgeon, <u>Streams in the Desert</u> by Lettie B. Cowman, and <u>The Christian's Secret of a Holy Life</u> by Hannah Whitall Smith. These devotional readings were written over a century ago, but are still applicable today.

I've also included a few contemporary devotionals, such as the <u>Celebrate Recovery Daily Devotional</u> by John Baker (a devotional written for people overcoming addictions) and <u>Amazing Grace</u> by Kenneth W. Osbeck (a devotional that looks at the lyrics of some of Christianity's most classic hymns).

There's even a *digital-only* devotional that Patty and I really like: <u>The Bible in One Year</u> by Nicky Gumbel.

The idea is to introduce you to the concept of using *a daily devotional reading* to accompany your study of the Bible. Do you *need* it? No. Can it be helpful? Certainly. Personally, I go through seasons of life where I read a devotional consistently, but then I have other seasons where I simply read the Bible (without the accompaniment of a devotional).

Seize The Word And Hold On No Matter What

The bottom line? It's my prayer that you will *seize the Word and hold on no matter what* by developing a daily habit of 1) reading God's Word, 2) making a personal application of what you read, and 3) reflecting on the truths you discover through a sampling of daily devotional readings.

ΔΔΔ

WHICH BIBLE TRANSLATION IS BEST?

This may come as shocking news to some, but the sixty-six books that comprise the Old and New Testaments of the Bible were not written by one man. Neither were they written in the course of one short season. And they certainly were not originally written in English!

In truth, the Bible was written over the course of 1,500 years, by forty different authors, in a wide variety of contexts—deserts, prisons, royal courts—and it was originally penned in three different languages (Greek, Hebrew, and Aramaic).

As you might imagine, it is rare to find someone who is fluent in any one of these ancient languages (let alone all three). It is just as rare to find a person who understands all the cultural nuances and writing habits of the various authors in the Bible.

Therefore, it is essential for English speakers to have an accurate and reliable English translation of the Bible. But, which translation is best?

WHICH TRANSLATION IS BEST?

Choosing an accurate, reliable, and readable translation is important—especially if you believe the Bible to be the very Word of God. But, how does one choose? There are over one hundred different English translations of the Bible!

Perhaps the most important aspect of choosing a Bible translation for yourself is to understand the two most basic approaches to translating the Bible: the *word-for-word* approach and the *thought-for-thought* approach.

WORDS OR THOUGHTS?

If you have ever attempted to learn a second language, you have likely discovered that learning another language is more than simply substituting a word in one language for a word in another language.

Why? Because each language has their own grammar, tense, structure, etc. That is to say, we cannot simply replace every word in an English sentence with a word from another language and hope that it properly *translates*. It just doesn't work that way.

For example, when an English speaker meets someone on the street, it's common to say *hello* or *hi.*

When Mandarin Chinese speakers meet each other, they also have a greeting. They say, 你好 *(nǐ hǎo)*. This Chinese greeting is the functional equivalent of our English *hello,* but the actual words they are speaking translate literally as *you good.*

So, which is the better English translation? *You good* or *hello?*

If we translate 你好 *(nǐ hǎo)* as *hello,* we are truly communicating the essence of what a Chinese speaker is saying. Unfortunately, we're also missing out on the good-natured sound of someone greeting us with a sweet, *you good!*

On the other hand, if we choose *you good* as the translation, we are being very literal, but it may sound odd since we don't greet one another by saying, *you good*, in English.

If you understand this small translation-dilemma, then you understand the task facing anyone who translates the Bible.

When presented with a similar task of translating *you good* or *hello* (but going from Greek to English, rather than Chinese to English) some Bible versions would choose *you good* while others would choose *hello.*

A Bible version that would choose *you good* is a *word-for-word* translation. A Bible version that would choose *hello* is a *thought-for-thought* translation.

Which approach is better? Word for Word? Thought for Thought?

Honestly, it's not a matter of one being better than the other; it's more about which one is the most understandable and helpful to you. To help you choose, I'll list a few of the pros and cons below.

WORD-FOR-WORD

Pros

1. Emphasizes faithfulness to the original text's literal *wording*.
2. Reduces the human-interpretation factor in Bible translation.
3. Attempts to replicate the original form and structure as closely as possible.

Cons

1. Can sound unnatural to how we actually communicate in English.
2. Cannot be 100% achieved, since translation is never completely word-for-word due to differences in grammar, tense, structure, etc.
3. Due to its rigidity, it can sometimes fail to translate the original meaning into the target language.

THOUGHT-FOR-THOUGHT

Pros

1. Emphasizes faithfulness to the original text's intended *meaning*.
2. More readable and easier to understand.
3. Sounds closer to how we actually communicate in modern English.

Cons

1. Cannot be 100% achieved, since it will invariably contain some of the translator's own bias.
2. More difficult for the reader to "see through" to the original text.
3. Can make in-depth original word study more difficult

YOU DON'T HAVE TO CHOOSE

Remember, it's not a matter of one version being better than the other; it's more about which version is the most understandable and helpful to you.

That said, what is most helpful to you can change from season to season.

I have found that reading a different version of the Bible can make truths *pop* to me that I have become accustomed to in other versions of the Bible. I've also discovered that when one version of the Bible doesn't make sense to me, another version will bring greater clarity.

It's perfectly ok to simultaneously use several versions along *The Translation Spectrum.*

THE TRANSLATION SPECTRUM

All English versions of the Bible fall somewhere along a translation spectrum. One end of this spectrum is *word-for-word* translations, and the other end is *thought-for-thought* translations.

Keep in mind that no English translation is 100% *word-for-word.* The only true word-for-word version of the Bible would be a Bible presented in the original Hebrew, Greek and Aramaic languages.

Also keep in mind that no English translation is 100% *thought-for-thought.* The only true thought-for-thought version of the Bible would be a Bible presented in the original Hebrew, Greek and Aramaic languages.

Below is a graphic showing several of the more popular English versions of the Bible and where they fall on the

Translation Spectrum.

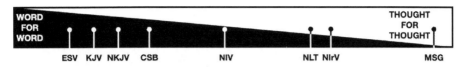

INTRODUCTIONS TO THE VERSIONS

Below you'll find a short description of each translation. Most of these descriptions are simply copied from the "About" section for each translation's information website.

In the chapters that follow, you'll have the chance to read several entire chapters of each of these Bible translations.

English Standard Version

From https://www.esv.org: The English Standard Version (ESV) is an essentially literal translation of the Bible in contemporary English. Created by a team of more than 100 leading evangelical scholars and pastors, the ESV Bible emphasizes word-for-word accuracy, literary excellence, and depth of meaning.

King James Version

From https://en.wikipedia.org/wiki/King_James_Version: The King James Version (KJV), also the King James Bible (KJB) and the Authorized Version (AV), is an English translation of the Christian Bible for the Church of England, which was commissioned in 1604 and published in 1611, by sponsorship of King James VI and I. . . . Noted for its "majesty of style", the King James Version has been described as one of the most important books in English culture and a driving force in the shaping of the

English-speaking world.

New King James Version

From https://www.thomasnelsonbibles.com/nkjv: The NKJV preserves the authority and accuracy, as well as the rhythm and beauty, of the original King James Version while making it understandable to current readers. The result is a Bible translation, scrupulously faithful to the original, yet truly updated to enhance its clarity and readability.

Christian Standard Bible

From https://csbible.com: The Christian Standard Bible presents the truth of God's Word with accuracy and clarity for today's readers, equipping them for lifelong discipleship. It's a Bible you can teach from with confidence and a Bible you can share with your neighbor hearing God's Word for the very first time.

New International Version

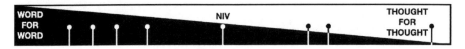

From https://www.biblica.com/niv-bible: Decades after the vision was cast, the New International Version (NIV) has become one of the most widely read translations in contemporary English. That's because the NIV delivers the very best combination of accuracy and readability. It's true to God's Word and true to the reader. There are plenty of things to wrestle with in the Bible. Your translation shouldn't be one of them.

New Living Translation

From https://www.tyndale.com/nlt: The New Living Translation combines the latest biblical scholarship with a clear, dynamic writing style that communicates God's Word powerfully to all who hear and read it. It renders the message of the original texts of Scripture into clear, contemporary English that was written to be read aloud. With a focus on clarity, The New Living Translation invites readers to go deeper into the biblical text to discover God's story for their lives and the world.

New International Reader's Version

From https://www.thenivbible.com/nirv/: When God first gave the Bible to his people, he used their languages. To this day, God wants us to understand his Word by spending time reading it in our own language and growing to know and love him more and more.

The New International Reader's Version (NIrV) opens the door for new Bible readers of all ages and abilities to understand God's Word. This version is based on the world's most-read and trusted modern English translation, the New International Version (NIV).

Wherever possible, the NIrV uses the text of the NIV but adapts it for reading at a third-grade level. In cases where phrases or words might be difficult to understand, words easier to understand have been used. And sentences are shorter, which is helpful for early readers and others who struggle with the English language. Throughout the translation, each verse has been meticulously evaluated in light of the meaning of the original languages in which the Bible was written.

The Message

The Message is the translation work of one man, Eugene Peterson. Here is what he says about the Message at https://messagebible.com/about/: If there is anything distinctive about The Message, perhaps it is because the text is shaped by the hand of a working pastor. For most of my adult life I have been given a primary responsibility for getting the message of the Bible into the lives of the men and women with whom I worked. I did it from the pulpit and lectern, in home Bible studies and at mountain retreats, through conversations in hospitals and nursing homes, over coffee in kitchens, and while strolling on an ocean beach. The Message grew from the soil of forty years of pastoral work.

LUKE 1

"He has filled the hungry with good things"

LUKE 1 (NIV)

New International version

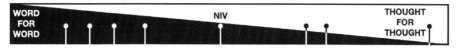

INTRODUCTION

Many have undertaken to draw up an account of the things that have been fulfilled among us,
2 just as they were handed down to us by those who from the first were eyewitnesses and servants of the word.
3 With this in mind, since I myself have carefully investigated everything from the beginning, I too decided to write an orderly account for you, most excellent Theophilus,
4 so that you may know the certainty of the things you have been taught.

THE BIRTH OF JOHN THE BAPTIST FORETOLD

5 In the time of Herod king of Judea there was a priest named Zechariah, who belonged to the priestly division of Abijah; his wife Elizabeth was also a descendant of Aaron.
6 Both of them were righteous in the sight of God, observing all the Lord's commands and decrees blamelessly.
7 But they were childless because Elizabeth was not able to conceive, and they were both very old.
8 Once when Zechariah's division was on duty and he was serving as priest before God,
9 he was chosen by lot, according to the custom of the priesthood, to go into the temple of the Lord and burn incense.

10 And when the time for the burning of incense came, all the assembled worshipers were praying outside.

11 Then an angel of the Lord appeared to him, standing at the right side of the altar of incense.

12 When Zechariah saw him, he was startled and was gripped with fear.

13 But the angel said to him: "Do not be afraid, Zechariah; your prayer has been heard. Your wife Elizabeth will bear you a son, and you are to call him John.

14 He will be a joy and delight to you, and many will rejoice because of his birth,

15 for he will be great in the sight of the Lord. He is never to take wine or other fermented drink, and he will be filled with the Holy Spirit even before he is born.

16 He will bring back many of the people of Israel to the Lord their God.

17 And he will go on before the Lord, in the spirit and power of Elijah, to turn the hearts of the parents to their children and the disobedient to the wisdom of the righteous—to make ready a people prepared for the Lord."

18 Zechariah asked the angel, "How can I be sure of this? I am an old man and my wife is well along in years."

19 The angel said to him, "I am Gabriel. I stand in the presence of God, and I have been sent to speak to you and to tell you this good news.

20 And now you will be silent and not able to speak until the day this happens, because you did not believe my words, which will come true at their appointed time."

21 Meanwhile, the people were waiting for Zechariah and wondering why he stayed so long in the temple.

22 When he came out, he could not speak to them. They realized he had seen a vision in the temple, for he kept making signs to them but remained unable to speak.

23 When his time of service was completed, he returned home.

24 After this his wife Elizabeth became pregnant and for five months remained in seclusion.

25 "The Lord has done this for me," she said. "In these days he has shown his favor and taken away my disgrace among the people."

THE BIRTH OF JESUS FORETOLD

26 In the sixth month of Elizabeth's pregnancy, God sent the angel Gabriel to Nazareth, a town in Galilee,

27 to a virgin pledged to be married to a man named Joseph, a descendant of David. The virgin's name was Mary.

28 The angel went to her and said, "Greetings, you who are highly favored! The Lord is with you."

29 Mary was greatly troubled at his words and wondered what kind of greeting this might be.

30 But the angel said to her, "Do not be afraid, Mary; you have found favor with God.

31 You will conceive and give birth to a son, and you are to call him Jesus.

32 He will be great and will be called the Son of the Most High. The Lord God will give him the throne of his father David,

33 and he will reign over Jacob's descendants forever; his kingdom will never end."

34 "How will this be," Mary asked the angel, "since I am a virgin?"

35 The angel answered, "The Holy Spirit will come on you, and the power of the Most High will overshadow you. So the holy one to be born will be called the Son of God.

36 Even Elizabeth your relative is going to have a child in her old age, and she who was said to be unable to conceive is in her sixth month.

37 For no word from God will ever fail."

38 "I am the Lord's servant," Mary answered. "May your word to me be fulfilled." Then the angel left her.

MARY VISITS ELIZABETH

39 At that time Mary got ready and hurried to a town in the hill

country of Judea,

40 where she entered Zechariah's home and greeted Elizabeth.

41 When Elizabeth heard Mary's greeting, the baby leaped in her womb, and Elizabeth was filled with the Holy Spirit.

42 In a loud voice she exclaimed: "Blessed are you among women, and blessed is the child you will bear!

43 But why am I so favored, that the mother of my Lord should come to me?

44 As soon as the sound of your greeting reached my ears, the baby in my womb leaped for joy.

45 Blessed is she who has believed that the Lord would fulfill his promises to her!"

MARY'S SONG

46 And Mary said: "My soul glorifies the Lord

47 and my spirit rejoices in God my Savior,

48 for he has been mindful of the humble state of his servant. From now on all generations will call me blessed,

49 for the Mighty One has done great things for me— holy is his name.

50 His mercy extends to those who fear him, from generation to generation.

51 He has performed mighty deeds with his arm; he has scattered those who are proud in their inmost thoughts.

52 He has brought down rulers from their thrones but has lifted up the humble.

53 He has filled the hungry with good things but has sent the rich away empty.

54 He has helped his servant Israel, remembering to be merciful

55 to Abraham and his descendants forever, just as he promised our ancestors."

56 Mary stayed with Elizabeth for about three months and then returned home.

THE BIRTH OF JOHN THE BAPTIST

57 When it was time for Elizabeth to have her baby, she gave birth to a son.

58 Her neighbors and relatives heard that the Lord had shown her great mercy, and they shared her joy.

59 On the eighth day they came to circumcise the child, and they were going to name him after his father Zechariah,

60 but his mother spoke up and said, "No! He is to be called John."

61 They said to her, "There is no one among your relatives who has that name."

62 Then they made signs to his father, to find out what he would like to name the child.

63 He asked for a writing tablet, and to everyone's astonishment he wrote, "His name is John."

64 Immediately his mouth was opened and his tongue set free, and he began to speak, praising God.

65 All the neighbors were filled with awe, and throughout the hill country of Judea people were talking about all these things.

66 Everyone who heard this wondered about it, asking, "What then is this child going to be?" For the Lord's hand was with him.

ZECHARIAH'S SONG

67 His father Zechariah was filled with the Holy Spirit and prophesied:

68 "Praise be to the Lord, the God of Israel, because he has come to his people and redeemed them.

69 He has raised up a horn of salvation for us in the house of his servant David

70 (as he said through his holy prophets of long ago),

71 salvation from our enemies and from the hand of all who hate us—

72 to show mercy to our ancestors and to remember his holy covenant,

73 the oath he swore to our father Abraham:

74 to rescue us from the hand of our enemies, and to enable us to serve him without fear

75 in holiness and righteousness before him all our days.

76 And you, my child, will be called a prophet of the Most High; for you will go on before the Lord to prepare the way for him,

77 to give his people the knowledge of salvation through the forgiveness of their sins,

78 because of the tender mercy of our God, by which the rising sun will come to us from heaven

79 to shine on those living in darkness and in the shadow of death, to guide our feet into the path of peace."

80 And the child grew and became strong in spirit; and he lived in the wilderness until he appeared publicly to Israel.

∆∆∆

S.O.A.P.

BIBLE STUDY METHOD

S.O.A.P. (which stand for Study, Observe, Apply, and Pray) is a simple method of Bible Study that you can use for any passage of scripture, including Luke 1.

1. Study

Study the scripture. You've already done this, but consider taking the time to reread Luke 2. Ask the Holy Spirit to illuminate what He would like you to see. Highlight words or phrases that stand out to you.

2. Observe

Make some observations. Who is this passage written by? To whom is this written to? Is there anything in this passage I've never noticed before? What is the context of this passage? (In other words, what comes before and after these verses)? Are there any specific words or phrases that stand out to me? Does this passage remind me of any other Bible passages?

3. Apply

For this step, ask yourself one simple question, "What is the Holy Spirit saying to me through these verses?" Take a moment to quiet yourself, and listen for God's voice. He may have something to say regarding your thoughts, your actions, your relationships, your plans, your dreams — and unless we consciously take the time to *just listen*, we may miss out on what he has to say.

4. Pray

Your prayer could include things like: thanking God for the truths that He highlighted during your study of the the Bible today, thanking him for what he helped you to observe, and asking for his help to apply these truths and observations to your life.

HIS BIRTH AND OUR NEW BIRTH

DEVOTIONAL READING

December 25 reading of Oswald Chambers, My Utmost for His Highest: Selections for the Year, (Grand Rapids, MI: Oswald Chambers Publications; Marshall Pickering, 1986).

"Therefore the Lord himself will give you a sign:
The virgin will conceive and give birth to a son, and
will call him Immanuel." (Isaiah 7:14, NIV)

His Birth In History

"...So the holy one to be born will be called
the Son of God." (Luke 1:35, NIV)

J esus Christ was born into this world, not from it. He did not evolve out of history; He came into history from the outside. Jesus Christ is not the best human being, He is a Being Who cannot be accounted for by the human race at all. He is not man becoming God, but God Incarnate, God coming into human flesh, coming into it from outside. His life is the Highest and the Holiest, entering in at the lowliest door. Our Lord's birth was an advent.

His Birth In Me

"Of whom I travail in birth again until Christ
be formed in you" (Gal. 4:19).

Just as Our Lord came into human history from outside, so He must come into me from outside. Have I allowed my personal human life to become a 'Bethlehem' for the Son of God? I cannot enter into the realm of the Kingdom of God unless I am born from above by a birth totally unlike natural birth.

"You must be born again." (John 3:7, NIV)

This is not a command, it is a foundation fact. The characteristic of the new birth is that I yield myself so completely to God that Christ is formed in me. Immediately Christ is formed in me, His nature begins to work through me.

God manifest in the flesh—that is what is made profoundly possible for you and me by the Redemption.

ΔΔΔ

LUKE 2

"I bring you good tidings of great joy"

LUKE 2 (KJV)

King James Version

CHRIST IS BORN

A nd it came to pass in those days, that there went out a decree from Caesar Augustus, that all the world should be taxed.

2 (And this taxing was first made when Cyrenius was governor of Syria.)

3 And all went to be taxed, every one into his own city.

4 And Joseph also went up from Galilee, out of the city of Nazareth, into Judaea, unto the city of David, which is called Bethlehem; (because he was of the house and lineage of David:)

5 To be taxed with Mary his espoused wife, being great with child.

6 And so it was, that, while they were there, the days were accomplished that she should be delivered.

7 And she brought forth her firstborn son, and wrapped him in swaddling clothes, and laid him in a manger; because there was no room for them in the inn.

THE ANGELS ANNOUNCE JESUS TO THE SHEPHERDS

8 And there were in the same country shepherds abiding in the field, keeping watch over their flock by night.

9 And, lo, the angel of the Lord came upon them, and the glory of

the Lord shone round about them: and they were sore afraid.

10 And the angel said unto them, Fear not: for, behold, I bring you good tidings of great joy, which shall be to all people.

11 For unto you is born this day in the city of David a Saviour, which is Christ the Lord.

12 And this shall be a sign unto you; Ye shall find the babe wrapped in swaddling clothes, lying in a manger.

13 And suddenly there was with the angel a multitude of the heavenly host praising God, and saying,

14 Glory to God in the highest, and on earth peace, good will toward men.

THE SHEPHERDS VISIT JESUS

15 And it came to pass, as the angels were gone away from them into heaven, the shepherds said one to another, Let us now go even unto Bethlehem, and see this thing which is come to pass, which the Lord hath made known unto us.

16 And they came with haste, and found Mary, and Joseph, and the babe lying in a manger.

17 And when they had seen it, they made known abroad the saying which was told them concerning this child.

18 And all they that heard it wondered at those things which were told them by the shepherds.

19 But Mary kept all these things, and pondered them in her heart.

20 And the shepherds returned, glorifying and praising God for all the things that they had heard and seen, as it was told unto them.

CHRIST IS CIRCUMCISED

21 And when eight days were accomplished for the circumcising of the child, his name was called JESUS, which was so named of the angel before he was conceived in the womb.

22 And when the days of her purification according to the law of Moses were accomplished, they brought him to Jerusalem, to present him to the Lord;

23 (As it is written in the law of the Lord, Every male that openeth the womb shall be called holy to the Lord;)

24 And to offer a sacrifice according to that which is said in the law of the Lord, A pair of turtledoves, or two young pigeons.

SIMEON'S PROPHECY

25 And, behold, there was a man in Jerusalem, whose name was Simeon; and the same man was just and devout, waiting for the consolation of Israel: and the Holy Ghost was upon him.

26 And it was revealed unto him by the Holy Ghost, that he should not see death, before he had seen the Lord's Christ.

27 And he came by the Spirit into the temple: and when the parents brought in the child Jesus, to do for him after the custom of the law,

28 Then took he him up in his arms, and blessed God, and said,

29 Lord, now lettest thou thy servant depart in peace, according to thy word:

30 For mine eyes have seen thy salvation,

31 Which thou hast prepared before the face of all people;

32 A light to lighten the Gentiles, and the glory of thy people

Israel.

33 And Joseph and his mother marvelled at those things which were spoken of him.

34 And Simeon blessed them, and said unto Mary his mother, Behold, this child is set for the fall and rising again of many in Israel; and for a sign which shall be spoken against;

35 (Yea, a sword shall pierce through thy own soul also,) that the thoughts of many hearts may be revealed.

ANNA'S TESTIMONY

36 And there was one Anna, a prophetess, the daughter of Phanuel, of the tribe of Aser: she was of a great age, and had lived with an husband seven years from her virginity;

37 And she was a widow of about fourscore and four years, which departed not from the temple, but served God with fastings and prayers night and day.

38 And she coming in that instant gave thanks likewise unto the Lord, and spake of him to all them that looked for redemption in Jerusalem.

JESUS RETURNS TO NAZARETH

39 And when they had performed all things according to the law of the Lord, they returned into Galilee, to their own city Nazareth.

40 And the child grew, and waxed strong in spirit, filled with wisdom: and the grace of God was upon him.

JESUS CELEBRATES THE PASSOVER

41 Now his parents went to Jerusalem every year at the feast of the passover.

42 And when he was twelve years old, they went up to Jerusalem after the custom of the feast.

43 And when they had fulfilled the days, as they returned, the child Jesus tarried behind in Jerusalem; and Joseph and his

mother knew not of it.

44 But they, supposing him to have been in the company, went a day's journey; and they sought him among their kinsfolk and acquaintance.

45 And when they found him not, they turned back again to Jerusalem, seeking him.

46 And it came to pass, that after three days they found him in the temple, sitting in the midst of the doctors, both hearing them, and asking them questions.

47 And all that heard him were astonished at his understanding and answers.

48 And when they saw him, they were amazed: and his mother said unto him, Son, why hast thou thus dealt with us? behold, thy father and I have sought thee sorrowing.

49 And he said unto them, How is it that ye sought me? wist ye not that I must be about my Father's business?

50 And they understood not the saying which he spake unto them.

JESUS GROWS IN WISDOM

51 And he went down with them, and came to Nazareth, and was subject unto them: but his mother kept all these sayings in her heart.

52 And Jesus increased in wisdom and stature, and in favour with God and man.

ΔΔΔ

R.E.A.P.

BIBLE STUDY METHOD

R.E.A.P. (which stand for Read, Examine, Apply, and Pray) is another method of Bible Study, which you will discover is very similar to S.O.A.P.

1. Read

You've already done this, but consider taking the time to *reread* Luke 2. Ask the Holy Spirit to illuminate what He would like you to see. Highlight words or phrases that stand out to you.

2. Examine

Ask yourself a few questions, such as: What is going on in the passage? What are the circumstances? Who are the main characters? What are the major themes? What is the context of this passage? (In other words, what comes before and after these verses)? Are there any specific words or phrases that stand out to me? Does this passage remind me of any other Bible passages?

3. Apply

Here's a few simple questions you can ask to help you apply Luke 2 (and any) passage: Is there a truth to believe? A sin to repent of? A promise to claim? A command to follow? What are things that need to change in light of this text? How will I live differently and be different because of what I just read? What is the Holy Spirit saying to me through these verses?

4. Pray

Your prayer could include things like: thanking God for the truths that He highlighted in your reading, thanking him for what he helped you to examine, and asking for his help to apply these to your life.

LOOK TO JESUS AS YOUR SAVIOUR

DEVOTIONAL READING

From the March 18 reading of bibleinoneyear.org by Nicky Gumbel

> "For unto you is born this day in the city of David a Savior, which is Christ the Lord." (Luke 2:11, KJV)

J esus is the Savior of the world. The angel had announced the birth of a 'Savior'. In this passage we see how on the eighth day he was named 'Jesus' which means 'the Lord saves'.

His parents take him to Jerusalem 'to present him to the Lord' and 'to offer a sacrifice according to that which is said in the law of the Lord' (vv.22–24). Jesus is the ultimate fulfillment of all the offerings and sacrifices we read about in the Old Testament.

1. Look To Jesus To Receive Peace.

Simeon takes Jesus in his arms and says to the Lord, "For mine eyes have seen thy salvation' (v.30). To see Jesus is to see salvation. Seeing Jesus gives Simeon 'peace' (v.29b).

2. Look To Jesus To See What God Is Like.

Jesus is a light that reveals God. He is 'A light to lighten the Gentiles.' (v.32a). It is impossible to know God unless he reveals himself to us. Yet God has done just that in Jesus. Jesus shows us what God is like. Jesus said, 'Anyone who has seen me has seen the father' (John 14:9). Jesus fully reveals God for everyone.

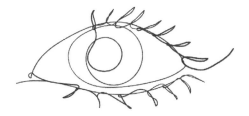

3. Look To Jesus For Grace And Truth.

Jesus is a light who brings glory: 'the glory of your people Israel' (Luke 2:32b). The word 'glory' speaks of God's excellence, beauty, greatness and perfection. God is glorious. Israel had glory because God had lived among them, first in the tabernacle in the desert, and then in the temple in Jerusalem.

With Jesus, Israel came to see God's glory in its truest and fullest sense. As John writes of Jesus, 'We have seen his glory, the glory of the one and only Son, who came from the Father, full of grace and truth' (John 1:14b). Jesus brings glory to Israel and to us, because Jesus is God coming to live among us.

Tragically though, many people reject the revelation and glory of God that we see in Jesus. Simeon prophesies about this, 'This child is destined to cause the falling and rising of many in Israel and to be a sign that will be spoken against, so that the thoughts of many hearts will be revealed' (Luke 2:34–35).

Being so closely associated with Jesus brings great blessing but also suffering. Maybe you have a family member, close friend, or someone else you really care about who is either antagonistic to Jesus or simply not interested. When we see people reject Jesus we get a tiny glimpse of what Mary must have experienced: 'And a sword will pierce your own soul too' (v.35).

This great suffering of Mary lay in the future. In the meantime, she had the joy of seeing Jesus growing up and becoming 'strong'. 'He was filled with wisdom, and the grace of God was on him' (v.40). 'Wisdom' and 'grace' are characteristics of the Savior that we should seek to imitate in our own lives.

Lord, give me eyes like Simeon to see your salvation in the world today. Give me grace and wisdom today for all my decisions, meetings and conversations.

LUKE 3

"Prepare the way of the Lord"

LUKE 3 (NKJV)

New King James Version

THE MINISTRY OF JOHN THE BAPTIST

N ow in the fifteenth year of the reign of Tiberius Caesar, Pontius Pilate being governor of Judea, Herod being tetrarch of Galilee, his brother Philip tetrarch of Iturea and the region of Trachonitis, and Lysanias tetrarch of Abilene,

2 while Annas and Caiaphas were high priests, the word of God came to John the son of Zacharias in the wilderness.

3 And he went into all the region around the Jordan, preaching a baptism of repentance for the remission of sins,

4 as it is written in the book of the words of Isaiah the prophet, saying: "The voice of one crying in the wilderness: 'Prepare the way of the Lord; Make His paths straight.

5 Every valley shall be filled And every mountain and hill brought low; The crooked places shall be made straight And the rough ways smooth;

6 And all flesh shall see the salvation of God.' "

7 Then he said to the multitudes that came out to be baptized by him, "Brood of vipers! Who warned you to flee from the wrath to come?

8 Therefore bear fruits worthy of repentance, and do not begin to say to yourselves, 'We have Abraham as our father.' For I say to you that God is able to raise up children to Abraham from these stones.

9 And even now the ax is laid to the root of the trees. Therefore every tree which does not bear good fruit is cut down and thrown into the fire."

10 So the people asked him, saying, "What shall we do then?"

11 He answered and said to them, "He who has two tunics, let him give to him who has none; and he who has food, let him do likewise."

12 Then tax collectors also came to be baptized, and said to him, "Teacher, what shall we do?"

13 And he said to them, "Collect no more than what is appointed for you."

14 Likewise the soldiers asked him, saying, "And what shall we do?" So he said to them, "Do not intimidate anyone or accuse falsely, and be content with your wages."

15 Now as the people were in expectation, and all reasoned in their hearts about John, whether he was the Christ or not,

16 John answered, saying to all, "I indeed baptize you with water; but One mightier than I is coming, whose sandal strap I am not worthy to loose. He will baptize you with the Holy Spirit and fire.

17 His winnowing fan is in His hand, and He will thoroughly clean out His threshing floor, and gather the wheat into His barn; but the chaff He will burn with unquenchable fire."

18 And with many other exhortations he preached to the people.

19 But Herod the tetrarch, being rebuked by him concerning Herodias, his brother Philip's wife, and for all the evils which Herod had done,

20 also added this, above all, that he shut John up in prison.

THE BAPTISM OF CHRIST

21 When all the people were baptized, it came to pass that Jesus also was baptized; and while He prayed, the heaven was opened.

22 And the Holy Spirit descended in bodily form like a dove upon Him, and a voice came from heaven which said, "You are My beloved Son; in You I am well pleased."

THE GENEALOGY OF CHRIST THROUGH MARY

23 Now Jesus Himself began His ministry at about thirty years of age, being (as was supposed) the son of Joseph, the son of Heli,

24 the son of Matthat, the son of Levi, the son of Melchi, the son of Janna, the son of Joseph,

25 the son of Mattathiah, the son of Amos, the son of Nahum, the son of Esli, the son of Naggai,

26 the son of Maath, the son of Mattathiah, the son of Semei, the son of Joseph, the son of Judah,

27 the son of Joannas, the son of Rhesa, the son of Zerubbabel, the son of Shealtiel, the son of Neri,

28 the son of Melchi, the son of Addi, the son of Cosam, the son of Elmodam, the son of Er,

29 the son of Jose, the son of Eliezer, the son of Jorim, the son of Matthat, the son of Levi,

30 the son of Simeon, the son of Judah, the son of Joseph, the son of Jonan, the son of Eliakim,

31 the son of Melea, the son of Menan, the son of Mattathah, the son of Nathan, the son of David,

32 the son of Jesse, the son of Obed, the son of Boaz, the son of Salmon, the son of Nahshon,

33 the son of Amminadab, the son of Ram, the son of Hezron, the son of Perez, the son of Judah,

34 the son of Jacob, the son of Isaac, the son of Abraham, the son of Terah, the son of Nahor,

35 the son of Serug, the son of Reu, the son of Peleg, the son of Eber, the son of Shelah,

36 the son of Cainan, the son of Arphaxad, the son of Shem, the son of Noah, the son of Lamech,

37 the son of Methuselah, the son of Enoch, the son of Jared, the son of Mahalalel, the son of Cainan,

38 the son of Enosh, the son of Seth, the son of Adam, the son of God.

ΔΔΔ

4R'S

BIBLE STUDY METHOD

Similar to both S.O.A.P and R.E.A.P, the 4R's are another simple method of Bible Study. The four R's are: Read, Reflect, Respond, Rest. Ready? Let's go!

1. Read

You've already done this, but consider taking the time to *reread* the passage. Ask the Holy Spirit to illuminate what He would like you to see. Highlight words or phrases that stand out to you.

2. Reflect

What is this passage saying to you? What did you hear, or what are you feeling or thinking? Consider asking a few of the questions we used in S.O.A.P and R.E.A.P, such as: what is the context of this passage? Are there any specific words or phrases that stand out to me? Does this passage remind me of any other Bible passages? Etc.

3. Respond

What is your response to what you've read? Ask yourself one simple question, "What is the Holy Spirit saying to me through these verses?" Take a moment to quiet yourself, and listen for God's voice. He may have something to say regarding your thoughts, your actions, your relationships, your plans, and your dreams.

4. Rest

Quietly ponder what you've read, and how you've chosen to respond — trusting God for the strength and courage necessary.

THE VOICE OF ONE CRYING IN THE WILDERNESS

DEVOTIONAL READING

January 3 reading of C. H. Spurgeon, Morning and Evening: Daily Readings (London: Passmore & Alabaster, 1896).

"The voice of one crying in the wilderness: 'Prepare the way of the Lord; Make His paths straight." (Luke 3:4, NKJV)

The voice crying in the wilderness demanded a way for the Lord, a way prepared, and a way prepared in the wilderness. I would be attentive to the Master's proclamation, and give him a road into my heart, cast up by gracious operations, through the desert of my nature. The four directions in the text must have my serious attention.

Every Valley Must Be Exalted.

Low and grovelling thoughts of God must be given up; doubting and despairing must be removed; and self-seeking and carnal delights must be forsaken. Across these deep valleys a glorious causeway of grace must be raised.

Every Mountain And Hill Shall Be Laid Low.

Proud creature-sufficiency, and boastful self-righteousness, must be levelled, to make a highway for the King of kings. Divine fellowship is never vouchsafed to haughty, highminded sinners. The Lord hath respect unto the lowly, and visits the contrite in heart, but the lofty are an abomination unto him. My soul, beseech the Holy Spirit to set thee right in this respect.

The Crooked Shall Be Made Straight.

The wavering heart must have a straight path of decision for God and holiness marked out for it. Double-minded men are strangers to the God of truth. My soul, take heed that thou be in all things honest and true, as in the sight of the heart-searching God.

The Rough Places Shall Be Made Smooth.

Stumbling-blocks of sin must be removed, and thorns and briers of rebellion must be uprooted. So great a visitor must not find miry ways and stony places when he comes to honour his favoured ones with his company.

> Oh that this evening the Lord may find in my heart a highway made ready by his grace, that he may make a triumphal progress through the utmost bounds of my soul, from the beginning of this year even to the end of it.

△△△

LUKE 4

"Man shall not live by bread alone"

LUKE 4 (ESV)

English Standard Version

THE TEMPTATION OF JESUS

A nd Jesus, full of the Holy Spirit, returned from the Jordan and was led by the Spirit in the wilderness

2 for forty days, being tempted by the devil. And he ate nothing during those days. And when they were ended, he was hungry.

3 The devil said to him, "If you are the Son of God, command this stone to become bread."

4 And Jesus answered him, "It is written, 'Man shall not live by bread alone.' "

5 And the devil took him up and showed him all the kingdoms of the world in a moment of time,

6 and said to him, "To you I will give all this authority and their glory, for it has been delivered to me, and I give it to whom I will.

7 If you, then, will worship me, it will all be yours."

8 And Jesus answered him, "It is written, " 'You shall worship the Lord your God, and him only shall you serve.' "

9 And he took him to Jerusalem and set him on the pinnacle of the temple and said to him, "If you are the Son of God, throw yourself down from here,

10 for it is written, " 'He will command his angels concerning you, to guard you,'

11 and " 'On their hands they will bear you up, lest you strike

your foot against a stone.' "

12 And Jesus answered him, "It is said, 'You shall not put the Lord your God to the test.' "

13 And when the devil had ended every temptation, he departed from him until an opportune time.

JESUS BEGINS HIS MINISTRY

14 And Jesus returned in the power of the Spirit to Galilee, and a report about him went out through all the surrounding country.

15 And he taught in their synagogues, being glorified by all.

JESUS REJECTED AT NAZARETH

16 And he came to Nazareth, where he had been brought up. And as was his custom, he went to the synagogue on the Sabbath day, and he stood up to read.

17 And the scroll of the prophet Isaiah was given to him. He unrolled the scroll and found the place where it was written,

18 "The Spirit of the Lord is upon me, because he has anointed me to proclaim good news to the poor. He has sent me to proclaim liberty to the captives and recovering of sight to the blind, to set at liberty those who are oppressed,

19 to proclaim the year of the Lord's favor."

20 And he rolled up the scroll and gave it back to the attendant and sat down. And the eyes of all in the synagogue were fixed on him.

21 And he began to say to them, "Today this Scripture has been fulfilled in your hearing."

22 And all spoke well of him and marveled at the gracious words that were coming from his mouth. And they said, "Is not this

Joseph's son?"

23 And he said to them, "Doubtless you will quote to me this proverb, ' "Physician, heal yourself." What we have heard you did at Capernaum, do here in your hometown as well.' "

24 And he said, "Truly, I say to you, no prophet is acceptable in his hometown.

25 But in truth, I tell you, there were many widows in Israel in the days of Elijah, when the heavens were shut up three years and six months, and a great famine came over all the land,

26 and Elijah was sent to none of them but only to Zarephath, in the land of Sidon, to a woman who was a widow.

27 And there were many lepers in Israel in the time of the prophet Elisha, and none of them was cleansed, but only Naaman the Syrian."

28 When they heard these things, all in the synagogue were filled with wrath.

29 And they rose up and drove him out of the town and brought him to the brow of the hill on which their town was built, so that they could throw him down the cliff.

30 But passing through their midst, he went away.

JESUS HEALS A MAN WITH AN UNCLEAN DEMON

31 And he went down to Capernaum, a city of Galilee. And he was teaching them on the Sabbath,

32 and they were astonished at his teaching, for his word possessed authority.

33 And in the synagogue there was a man who had the spirit of an unclean demon, and he cried out with a loud voice,

34 "Ha! What have you to do with us, Jesus of Nazareth? Have you come to destroy us? I know who you are—the Holy One of God."

35 But Jesus rebuked him, saying, "Be silent and come out of him!" And when the demon had thrown him down in their midst, he came out of him, having done him no harm.

36 And they were all amazed and said to one another, "What is this word? For with authority and power he commands the unclean spirits, and they come out!"

37 And reports about him went out into every place in the surrounding region.

JESUS HEALS MANY

38 And he arose and left the synagogue and entered Simon's house. Now Simon's mother-in-law was ill with a high fever, and they appealed to him on her behalf.

39 And he stood over her and rebuked the fever, and it left her, and immediately she rose and began to serve them.

40 Now when the sun was setting, all those who had any who were sick with various diseases brought them to him, and he laid his hands on every one of them and healed them.

41 And demons also came out of many, crying, "You are the Son of God!" But he rebuked them and would not allow them to speak, because they knew that he was the Christ.

JESUS PREACHES IN SYNAGOGUES

42 And when it was day, he departed and went into a desolate place. And the people sought him and came to him, and would have kept him from leaving them,

43 but he said to them, "I must preach the good news of the kingdom of God to the other towns as well; for I was sent for this purpose."

44 And he was preaching in the synagogues of Judea.

ΔΔΔ

C.O.R.E.

BIBLE STUDY METHOD

C.O.R.E. is a method I (Paul) personally created; I use it nearly every time I preach or teach the Bible. It's based on a book by Ken Davis called, "Secrets of Dynamic Communication."

1. Catalytic Question

Consider taking a moment to reread Luke 4. As you do, see if there is a big question that Luke chapter 4 seems to be answering. This big question is your *Catalytic* Question. By *catalytic*, I mean it's the kind of question that sparks more ideas and thoughts.

2. Objective Sentence

The objective sentence is your *answer* to the catalytic question, which is based on what you just read in Luke 4. For example, if your catalytic question is, "What did Jesus come to do?" Your objective sentence might say, *"Jesus came to transform lives in (at least) five ways."*

3. Rationale

The Rationale is where you provide more details to the objective sentence. So, to continue our example from above, our rationale for saying that, "Jesus came to transform lives in five ways" could be something like: *1) He proclaims good news to the poor, 2) He proclaims liberty to the captives, 3) He gives sight to the blind, 4) He liberates those who are oppressed and 5) He proclaims the year of the Lord's favor.*

4. Express Thanks

Take a moment to express thanks to God for what he has shown you in his Word today.

ENCOUNTERING TEMPTATION

DEVOTIONAL READING

April 12 Reading of Lettie B. Cowman, Streams in the Desert (Los Angeles, CA: The Oriental Missionary Society, 1925), 113–114.

"And Jesus, full of the Holy Spirit, returned from the Jordan and was led by the Spirit in the wilderness for forty days, being tempted by the devil…" (Luke 4:1–2, ESV)

JESUS was full of the Holy Ghost, and yet He was tempted. Temptation often comes upon a man with its strongest power when he is nearest to God. As someone has said, "The devil aims high." He got one apostle to say he did not even know Christ.

Very few men have such conflicts with the devil as Martin Luther had. Why? Because Martin Luther was going to shake the very kingdom of hell. Oh, what conflicts John Bunyan had!

"If a man has much of the Spirit of God, he will have great conflicts with the tempter. God permits temptation because it does for us what the storms do for the oaks—it roots us; and what the fire does for the paintings on the porcelain—it makes them permanent.

You never know that you have a grip on Christ, or that He has a grip on you, as well as when the devil is using all his force to attract you from Him; then you feel the pull of Christ's right hand." —Selected.

"Extraordinary afflictions are not always the punishment of extraordinary sins, but sometimes the trial of extraordinary graces. God hath many sharp-cutting instruments, and rough files for the polishing of His jewels; and those He especially loves, and means to make the most resplendent, He hath oftenest His tools upon."—Archbishop Leighton.

"I bear my willing witness that I owe more to the fire, and the hammer, and the file, than to anything else in my Lord's workshop. I sometimes question whether I have ever learned anything except through the rod. When my schoolroom is darkened, I see most."—C. H. Spurgeon.

LUKE 5

"Follow me"

LUKE 5 (CSB)

Christian Standard Bible

THE FIRST DISCIPLES

As the crowd was pressing in on Jesus to hear God's word, he was standing by Lake Gennesaret. 2 He saw two boats at the edge of the lake; the fishermen had left them and were washing their nets.

3 He got into one of the boats, which belonged to Simon, and asked him to put out a little from the land. Then he sat down and was teaching the crowds from the boat.

4 When he had finished speaking, he said to Simon, "Put out into deep water and let down your nets for a catch."

5 "Master," Simon replied, "we've worked hard all night long and caught nothing. But if you say so, I'll let down the nets."

6 When they did this, they caught a great number of fish, and their nets began to tear.

7 So they signaled to their partners in the other boat to come and help them; they came and filled both boats so full that they began to sink.

8 When Simon Peter saw this, he fell at Jesus's knees and said, "Go away from me, because I'm a sinful man, Lord!"

9 For he and all those with him were amazed at the catch of fish they had taken,

10 and so were James and John, Zebedee's sons, who were Simon's partners. "Don't be afraid," Jesus told Simon. "From now

on you will be catching people."

11 Then they brought the boats to land, left everything, and followed him.

A MAN CLEANSED

12 While he was in one of the towns, a man was there who had leprosy all over him. He saw Jesus, fell facedown, and begged him: "Lord, if you are willing, you can make me clean."

13 Reaching out his hand, Jesus touched him, saying, "I am willing; be made clean," and immediately the leprosy left him.

14 Then he ordered him to tell no one: "But go and show yourself to the priest, and offer what Moses commanded for your cleansing as a testimony to them."

15 But the news about him spread even more, and large crowds would come together to hear him and to be healed of their sicknesses.

16 Yet he often withdrew to deserted places and prayed.

THE SON OF MAN FORGIVES AND HEALS

17 On one of those days while he was teaching, Pharisees and teachers of the law were sitting there who had come from every village of Galilee and Judea, and also from Jerusalem. And the Lord's power to heal was in him.

18 Just then some men came, carrying on a stretcher a man who was paralyzed. They tried to bring him in and set him down before him.

19 Since they could not find a way to bring him in because of the crowd, they went up on the roof and lowered him on the stretcher through the roof tiles into the middle of the crowd before Jesus.

20 Seeing their faith he said, "Friend, your sins are forgiven."

21 Then the scribes and the Pharisees began to think to themselves: "Who is this man who speaks blasphemies? Who can forgive sins but God alone?"

22 But perceiving their thoughts, Jesus replied to them, "Why are you thinking this in your hearts?

23 Which is easier: to say, 'Your sins are forgiven,' or to say, 'Get up and walk'?

24 But so that you may know that the Son of Man has authority on earth to forgive sins"—he told the paralyzed man, "I tell you: Get up, take your stretcher, and go home."

25 Immediately he got up before them, picked up what he had been lying on, and went home glorifying God.

26 Then everyone was astounded, and they were giving glory to God. And they were filled with awe and said, "We have seen incredible things today."

THE CALL OF LEVI

27 After this, Jesus went out and saw a tax collector named Levi sitting at the tax office, and he said to him, "Follow me."

28 So, leaving everything behind, he got up and began to follow him.

29 Then Levi hosted a grand banquet for him at his house. Now there was a large crowd of tax collectors and others who were guests with them.

30 But the Pharisees and their scribes were complaining to his disciples, "Why do you eat and drink with tax collectors and sinners?"

31 Jesus replied to them, "It is not those who are healthy who

need a doctor, but those who are sick.

32 I have not come to call the righteous, but sinners to repentance."

A QUESTION ABOUT FASTING

33 Then they said to him, "John's disciples fast often and say prayers, and those of the Pharisees do the same, but yours eat and drink."

34 Jesus said to them, "You can't make the wedding guests fast while the groom is with them, can you?

35 But the time will come when the groom will be taken away from them—then they will fast in those days."

36 He also told them a parable: "No one tears a patch from a new garment and puts it on an old garment. Otherwise, not only will he tear the new, but also the piece from the new garment will not match the old.

37 And no one puts new wine into old wineskins. Otherwise, the new wine will burst the skins, it will spill, and the skins will be ruined.

38 No, new wine is put into fresh wineskins.

39 And no one, after drinking old wine, wants new, because he says, 'The old is better.' "

△△△

DISCOVERY

BIBLE STUDY METHOD

A Discovery Bible Study (DBS) is question-based Bible study that encourages the discovery of the Bible, obeying what is learned, and then sharing it with others.

Read

Begin by reading (and rereading) the passage, and then answer the following questions.

Questions

1. What does this scripture tell me about God and/or His plan?

2. What does this scripture tell me about people?

3. If this scripture is truly from God, how will I apply and obey it? (Begin your answer by saying, "I will...")

4. Who needs to hear this scripture, and when will I share it?

PUTTING THE LORD FIRST

DEVOTIONAL READING

August 2 and August 25 reading of Samuel G. Hardman and Dwight Lyman Moody, Thoughts for the Quiet Hour (Willow Grove, PA: Woodlawn Electronic Publishing, 1997).

"He got into one of the boats...and...sat down..." (Luke 5:3, CSB)

When Jesus sits in the ship everything is in its right place. The cargo is in the hold, not in the heart. Cares and gains, fears and losses, yesterday's failure and today's success do not thrust themselves in between us and His presence. The heart cleaves to Him.

"Goodness and mercy shall follow me", sang the Psalmist. Alas, when the goodness and mercy come before us, and our blessings shut Jesus from view! Here is the blessed order—the Lord ever first, I following Him, His goodness and mercy following me. — Mark Guy Pearse

"...nevertheless at thy word..." (Luke 5:5, KJV)

Oh, what a blessed formula for us! This path of mine is dark, mysterious, perplexing; nevertheless, at Thy word I will go forward. This trial of mine is cutting, sore for flesh and blood to bear. It is hard to breathe through a broken heart, Thy will be done. But, nevertheless, at Thy word I will say, Even so, Father!

This besetting habit, or infirmity, or sin of mine, is difficult to crucify. It has become part of myself—a second nature; to be severed from it would be like the cutting off of a right hand, or the plucking out of a right eye; nevertheless, at Thy word I will lay aside every weight; this idol I will utterly abolish.

This righteousness of mine it is hard to ignore; all these virtues, and amiabilities, and natural graces, it is hard to believe that they dare not in any way be mixed up in the matter of my salvation; and that I am to receive all from first to last as the gift of God, through Jesus Christ my Lord. Nevertheless, at Thy word I will count all but loss for the excellency of His knowledge. — Macduff

LUKE 6

"Do to others as you would like them to do to you"

LUKE 6 (NLT)

New Living Translation

A DISCUSSION ABOUT THE SABBATH

One Sabbath day as Jesus was walking through some grainfields, his disciples broke off heads of grain, rubbed off the husks in their hands, and ate the grain.

2 But some Pharisees said, "Why are you breaking the law by harvesting grain on the Sabbath?"

3 Jesus replied, "Haven't you read in the Scriptures what David did when he and his companions were hungry?

4 He went into the house of God and broke the law by eating the sacred loaves of bread that only the priests can eat. He also gave some to his companions."

5 And Jesus added, "The Son of Man is Lord, even over the Sabbath."

JESUS HEALS ON THE SABBATH

6 On another Sabbath day, a man with a deformed right hand was in the synagogue while Jesus was teaching.

7 The teachers of religious law and the Pharisees watched Jesus closely. If he healed the man's hand, they planned to accuse him of working on the Sabbath.

8 But Jesus knew their thoughts. He said to the man with the deformed hand, "Come and stand in front of everyone." So the man came forward.

9 Then Jesus said to his critics, "I have a question for you. Does the law permit good deeds on the Sabbath, or is it a day for doing evil? Is this a day to save life or to destroy it?"

10 He looked around at them one by one and then said to the man, "Hold out your hand." So the man held out his hand, and it was restored!

11 At this, the enemies of Jesus were wild with rage and began to discuss what to do with him.

JESUS CHOOSES THE TWELVE APOSTLES

12 One day soon afterward Jesus went up on a mountain to pray, and he prayed to God all night.

13 At daybreak he called together all of his disciples and chose twelve of them to be apostles. Here are their names:

14 Simon (whom he named Peter), Andrew (Peter's brother), James, John, Philip, Bartholomew,

15 Matthew, Thomas, James (son of Alphaeus), Simon (who was called the zealot),

16 Judas (son of James), Judas Iscariot (who later betrayed him).

CROWDS FOLLOW JESUS

17 When they came down from the mountain, the disciples stood with Jesus on a large, level area, surrounded by many of his followers and by the crowds. There were people from all over Judea and from Jerusalem and from as far north as the seacoasts of Tyre and Sidon.

18 They had come to hear him and to be healed of their diseases; and those troubled by evil spirits were healed.

19 Everyone tried to touch him, because healing power went out from him, and he healed everyone.

THE BEATITUDES

20 Then Jesus turned to his disciples and said, "God blesses you who are poor, for the Kingdom of God is yours.

21 God blesses you who are hungry now, for you will be satisfied. God blesses you who weep now, for in due time you will laugh.

22 What blessings await you when people hate you and exclude you and mock you and curse you as evil because you follow the Son of Man.

23 When that happens, be happy! Yes, leap for joy! For a great reward awaits you in heaven. And remember, their ancestors treated the ancient prophets that same way.

SORROWS FORETOLD

24 "What sorrow awaits you who are rich, for you have your only happiness now.

25 What sorrow awaits you who are fat and prosperous now, for a time of awful hunger awaits you. What sorrow awaits you who laugh now, for your laughing will turn to mourning and sorrow.

26 What sorrow awaits you who are praised by the crowds, for their ancestors also praised false prophets.

LOVE FOR ENEMIES

27 "But to you who are willing to listen, I say, love your enemies! Do good to those who hate you.

28 Bless those who curse you. Pray for those who hurt you.

29 If someone slaps you on one cheek, offer the other cheek also. If someone demands your coat, offer your shirt also.

30 Give to anyone who asks; and when things are taken away from you, don't try to get them back.

31 Do to others as you would like them to do to you.

32 "If you love only those who love you, why should you get credit for that? Even sinners love those who love them!

33 And if you do good only to those who do good to you, why should you get credit? Even sinners do that much!

34 And if you lend money only to those who can repay you, why should you get credit? Even sinners will lend to other sinners for a full return.

35 "Love your enemies! Do good to them. Lend to them without expecting to be repaid. Then your reward from heaven will be very great, and you will truly be acting as children of the Most High, for he is kind to those who are unthankful and wicked.

36 You must be compassionate, just as your Father is compassionate.

DO NOT JUDGE OTHERS

37 "Do not judge others, and you will not be judged. Do not condemn others, or it will all come back against you. Forgive others, and you will be forgiven.

38 Give, and you will receive. Your gift will return to you in full—pressed down, shaken together to make room for more, running over, and poured into your lap. The amount you give will determine the amount you get back."

39 Then Jesus gave the following illustration: "Can one blind person lead another? Won't they both fall into a ditch?

40 Students are not greater than their teacher. But the student who is fully trained will become like the teacher.

41 "And why worry about a speck in your friend's eye when you have a log in your own?

42 How can you think of saying, 'Friend, let me help you get rid of that speck in your eye,' when you can't see past the log in your own eye? Hypocrite! First get rid of the log in your own eye; then you will see well enough to deal with the speck in your friend's eye.

THE TREE AND ITS FRUIT

43 "A good tree can't produce bad fruit, and a bad tree can't produce good fruit.

44 A tree is identified by its fruit. Figs are never gathered from thornbushes, and grapes are not picked from bramble bushes.

45 A good person produces good things from the treasury of a good heart, and an evil person produces evil things from the treasury of an evil heart. What you say flows from what is in your heart.

BUILDING ON A SOLID FOUNDATION

46 "So why do you keep calling me 'Lord, Lord!' when you don't do what I say?

47 I will show you what it's like when someone comes to me, listens to my teaching, and then follows it.

48 It is like a person building a house who digs deep and lays the foundation on solid rock. When the floodwaters rise and break against that house, it stands firm because it is well built.

49 But anyone who hears and doesn't obey is like a person who builds a house right on the ground, without a foundation. When the floods sweep down against that house, it will collapse into a heap of ruins."

ΔΔΔ

C.U.B.E.

BIBLE STUDY METHOD

*Another acrostic to help you study the Bible! The letters of
C.U.B.E. stand for Circle, Underline, Bracket, and Express.*

(Circle)

Read Luke 6 again (out loud) but this time look for anything
that has to do with God (Father, Son, or Holy Spirit). Put a
(circle) around every mention of his name, including pronouns
referring to him.

Underline

Read Luke 6 once again, but this time around look for
statements that talk about how a follower of Jesus *should live*.
When you find such a statement, underline it.

[Bracket]

Read Luke 6 one more time, but this time look for statements that talk about how a believer should *not* live. When you encounter such a statement, put a set of [brackets] around it.

Express

Congratulations! You have just read the same passage of scripture 4 times. By (circling), underlining, and [bracketing] you have involved 3 of your senses: sight, sound, and touch. Take a moment to express your worship and gratitude to God for anything he has revealed to you during your study.

GIVING AND ACCEPTING FORGIVENESS

DEVOTIONAL READING

Day 20 reading of John Baker and Johnny Baker, Celebrate Recovery Daily Devotional: 366 Devotionals (Grand Rapids, MI: Zondervan, 2013).

"Do to others as you would like them to do to you." (Luke 6:31, NLT)

A guy once told me, "John, you won't catch me getting ulcers. I just take things as they come. I don't ever hold a grudge, not even against people who have done things to me that I'll never forgive." Right! Forgiveness is a beautiful idea until we have to practice it!

There are a lot of jokes about forgiveness, but forgiveness is not something that those of us in recovery can take lightly, because forgiveness is clearly God's prescription for the broken. No matter how great the offense or abuse, forgiveness lies along the path to healing.

We all know that one of the roots of compulsive behavior is buried pain. So facing our past and forgiving ourselves and those who have hurt us, as well as making amends for the pain that we have caused others, is the only lasting solution. Forgiveness breaks the cycle! It doesn't settle all the questions of blame, justice, or fairness, but it does allow relationships to heal and possibly start over.

In order to be completely free from our resentments, anger, fears, shame, and guilt, we need to give and accept *forgiveness* in all areas of our lives. If we do not, our recovery will remain incomplete. God wants much more than that for us. He wants us to walk in wholeness, ready to follow the path he planned for us before the beginning of time.

Father, what a gift I've found in forgiving and receiving forgiveness. Thank you for your goodness to me. In Jesus' name, Amen.

LUKE 7

"God has come to help his people"

LUKE 7 (NIRV)

New International Reader's Version

J esus finished saying all those things to the people. Then he entered Capernaum. There the servant of a Roman commander was sick and about to die. His master thought highly of him. The commander heard about Jesus. So he sent some elders of the Jews to him. He told them to ask Jesus to come and heal his servant. They came to Jesus and begged him, "This man deserves to have you do this. He loves our nation and has built our synagogue."

So Jesus went with them. When Jesus came near the house, the Roman commander sent friends to him. He told them to say, "Lord, don't trouble yourself. I am not good enough to have you come into my house. That is why I did not even think I was fit to come to you. But just say the word, and my servant will be healed. I myself am a man who is under authority. And I have soldiers who obey my orders. I tell this one, 'Go,' and he goes. I tell that one, 'Come,' and he comes. I say to my servant, 'Do this,' and he does it."

When Jesus heard this, he was amazed at him. He turned to the crowd that was following him. He said, "I tell you, even in Israel I have not found anyone whose faith is so strong." Then the men who had been sent to Jesus returned to the house. They found that the servant was healed.

Some time later, Jesus went to a town called Nain. His disciples and a large crowd went along with him. He approached the town gate. Just then, a dead person was being carried out. He was the only son of his mother. She was a widow. A large crowd from the town was with her. When the Lord saw her, he felt sorry for her. So he said, "Don't cry." Then he went up and touched the coffin. Those carrying it stood still. Jesus said, "Young man, I say to you, get up!" The dead man sat up and began to talk. Then Jesus gave him back to his mother.

The people were all filled with wonder and praised God. "A great prophet has appeared among us," they said. "God has come to help his people." This news about Jesus spread all through Judea and the whole country.

John's disciples told him about all these things. So he chose two of them. He sent them to the Lord. They were to ask Jesus, "Are you the one who was supposed to come? Or should we look for someone else?"

The men came to Jesus. They said, "John the Baptist sent us to ask you, 'Are you the one who was supposed to come? Or should we look for someone else?' "

At that very time Jesus healed many people. They had illnesses, sicknesses and evil spirits. He also gave sight to many who were blind. So Jesus replied to the messengers, "Go back to John. Tell him what you have seen and heard. Blind people receive sight. Disabled people walk. Those who have skin diseases are healed. Deaf people hear. Those who are dead are raised to life. And the good news is preached to those who are poor. Blessed are those who do not give up their faith because of me."

So John's messengers left. Then Jesus began to speak to the crowd about John. He said, "What did you go out into the desert to see? Tall grass waving in the wind? If not, what did you go out to see? A man dressed in fine clothes? No. Those who wear fine clothes and have many expensive things are in palaces. Then what did you go out to see? A prophet? Yes, I tell you, and more than a prophet. He is the one written about in Scripture. It says, 'I will send my messenger ahead of you. He will prepare your way for you.' I tell you, no one more important than John has ever been born. But the least important person in God's kingdom is more important than he is."

All the people who heard Jesus' words agreed that God's way was right. Even the tax collectors agreed. These people had all been baptized by John. But the Pharisees and the authorities on the law did not accept God's purpose for themselves. They had not been baptized by John.

"What can I compare today's people to?" Jesus asked. "What are they like? They are like children sitting in the market place and calling out to each other. They say, 'We played a flute for you. But you didn't dance. We sang a funeral song. But you didn't cry.' That is how it has been with John the Baptist. When he came to you, he didn't eat bread or drink wine. And you say, 'He has a demon.' But when the Son of Man came, he ate and drank as you do. And you say, 'This fellow is always eating and drinking far too much. He's a friend of tax collectors and "sinners." ' All who follow wisdom prove that wisdom is right."

One of the Pharisees invited Jesus to have dinner with him. So he went to the Pharisee's house. He took his place at the table. There was a woman in that town who had lived a sinful life. She learned that Jesus was eating at the Pharisee's house. So she came with a special sealed jar of perfume. She stood behind Jesus and cried at his feet. She began to wet his feet with her tears. Then she wiped them with her hair. She kissed them and poured perfume on them. The Pharisee who had invited Jesus saw this. He said to himself, "If this man were a prophet, he would know who is touching him. He would know what kind of woman she is. She is a sinner!"

Jesus answered him, "Simon, I have something to tell you."

"Tell me, teacher," he said.

"Two people owed money to a certain lender. One owed him 500 silver coins. The other owed him 50 silver coins. Neither of them had the money to pay him back. So he let them go without paying. Which of them will love him more?"

Simon replied, "I suppose the one who owed the most money." "You are right," Jesus said.

Then he turned toward the woman. He said to Simon, "Do you see this woman? I came into your house. You did not give me any water to wash my feet. But she wet my feet with her tears and wiped them with her hair. You did not give me a kiss. But this woman has not stopped kissing my feet since I came in. You did not put any olive oil on my head. But she has poured perfume on my feet. So I tell you this. Her many sins have been forgiven. She has loved a lot. But the one who has been forgiven little loves only a little."

Then Jesus said to her, "Your sins are forgiven."

The other guests began to talk about this among themselves. They said, "Who is this who even forgives sins?"

Jesus said to the woman, "Your faith has saved you. Go in peace."

ΔΔΔ

MANUSCRIPT

BIBLE STUDY METHOD

The Manuscript Bible study method is used widely by Intervarsity Christian Fellowship to help students dig into Scripture.

Introduction

You may have noticed that the previous chapter (Luke 7) didn't include any paragraph headings or verse numbers. This is the distinguishing characteristic of a Manuscript Bible Study.

In a Manuscript study, you start with the basic text of the Bible with nothing else added—since chapter numbers, verse numbers, punctuation, and paragraph headings were actually added years later to our translations (English and other language translations) to make it easier to navigate the Bible. (The original Greek and Hebrew documents simply didn't have these features). Here's how it works:

Look For The W's:

Who is involved? *When* did it happen? *Where* is it happening? *What* is taking place? Ask yourself a few *why* questions regarding what the chapter is about.

Mark It Up!

Use a variety of colored pens and pencils to mark up the chapter. (You may want to employ a bit of the C.U.B.E method we looked at with Luke 6, and perhaps throw in a few other shapes—such as squiggly lines or smily faces—that make sense to you). Don't worry about getting it "right," just mark it up.

Reflect, Pray, Act:

How does what you're reading and studying apply to you and where you are with God, others, etc.?

LOVE, PRAISE, FORGIVENESS

DEVOTIONAL READING

*August 10 reading of John D. Barry and Rebecca Kruyswijk,
Connect the Testaments: A One-Year Daily Devotional with Bible
Reading Plan (Bellingham, WA: Lexham Press, 2012).*

"So I tell you this. Her many sins have been forgiven.
She has loved a lot. But the one who has been forgiven
little loves only a little." (Luke 7:47, NiRV)

Our praise for God is often directly connected to accepting and confessing our brokenness. Our capacity to love Him is tied to the realization of how much He has forgiven us.

The woman in Luke 7 who anointed Jesus' feet is described with one phrase: She was a sinner. We're not given clarifying detail, but we do know her sin was notorious and, as a result, she was marginalized by society. She was not only weighed down by her sin; her public identity was grounded in it, and she could not hide it. She knew that she needed to receive forgiveness from the only one who could provide it. Her necessity made her bold: She came to Simon the Pharisee's house to wash and anoint Jesus' feet.

Her behavior created quite a spectacle. Simon the Pharisee was quick to condemn her actions and question Jesus' decision to show her compassion. But Jesus turned the tables on him.

While the woman was aware of her brokenness—and was all the more grateful for forgiveness—Simon ran with those who had built up a charade of holiness.

Jesus told Simon, "So I tell you this. Her many sins have been forgiven. She has loved a lot. But the one who has been forgiven little loves only a little." (Luke 7:47, NiRV)

Our praise for Jesus—the way we speak of Him and the way we speak of our sin and forgiveness—is a reflection of the state of our hearts. Because our hearts are inclined to be prideful, it's often easier for us to defend our sin than to confess it. It's easier to go about our religious activities while rationalizing our sin. But unless we drop the charade and confess the true state of our hearts, we'll never honor Him as we should.

Do you "love little"? What holds you back from expressing praise?

LUKE 8

"Seize the Word and hold on no matter what"

LUKE 8 (MSG)

The Message

SPREADING THE MESSAGE

He continued according to plan, traveled to town after town, village after village, preaching God's kingdom, spreading the Message. The Twelve were with him. There were also some women in their company who had been healed of various evil afflictions and illnesses: Mary, the one called Magdalene, from whom seven demons had gone out; Joanna, wife of Chuza, Herod's manager; and Susanna—along with many others who used their considerable means to provide for the company.

THE STORY OF THE SEEDS

4-8 As they went from town to town, a lot of people joined in and traveled along. He addressed them, using this story: "A farmer went out to sow his seed. Some of it fell on the road; it was tramped down and the birds ate it. Other seed fell in the gravel; it sprouted, but withered because it didn't have good roots. Other seed fell in the weeds; the weeds grew with it and strangled it. Other seed fell in rich earth and produced a bumper crop.

"Are you listening to this? Really listening?"

9 His disciples asked, "Why did you tell this story?"

10 He said, "You've been given insight into God's kingdom—you know how it works. There are others who need stories. But even

with stories some of them aren't going to get it: Their eyes are open but don't see a thing, Their ears are open but don't hear a thing.

11-12 "This story is about some of those people. The seed is the Word of God. The seeds on the road are those who hear the Word, but no sooner do they hear it than the Devil snatches it from them so they won't believe and be saved.

13 "The seeds in the gravel are those who hear with enthusiasm, but the enthusiasm doesn't go very deep. It's only another fad, and the moment there's trouble it's gone.

14 "And the seed that fell in the weeds—well, these are the ones who hear, but then the seed is crowded out and nothing comes of it as they go about their lives worrying about tomorrow, making money, and having fun.

15 "But the seed in the good earth—these are the good-hearts who seize the Word and hold on no matter what, sticking with it until there's a harvest.

MISERS OF WHAT YOU HEAR

16-18 "No one lights a lamp and then covers it with a washtub or shoves it under the bed. No, you set it up on a lamp stand so those who enter the room can see their way. We're not keeping secrets; we're telling them. We're not hiding things; we're bringing everything out into the open. So be careful that you don't become misers of what you hear. Generosity begets generosity. Stinginess impoverishes."

19-20 His mother and brothers showed up but couldn't get through to him because of the crowd. He was given the message, "Your mother and brothers are standing outside wanting to see you."

21 He replied, "My mother and brothers are the ones who hear and do God's Word. Obedience is thicker than blood."

22-24 One day he and his disciples got in a boat. "Let's cross the lake," he said. And off they went. It was smooth sailing, and he fell asleep. A terrific storm came up suddenly on the lake. Water poured in, and they were about to capsize. They woke Jesus: "Master, Master, we're going to drown!"

Getting to his feet, he told the wind, "Silence!" and the waves, "Quiet down!" They did it. The lake became smooth as glass.

25 Then he said to his disciples, "Why can't you trust me?"

They were in absolute awe, staggered and stammering, "Who is this, anyway? He calls out to the winds and sea, and they do what he tells them!"

THE MADMAN AND THE PIGS

26-29 They sailed on to the country of the Gerasenes, directly opposite Galilee. As he stepped out onto land, a madman from town met him; he was a victim of demons. He hadn't worn clothes for a long time, nor lived at home; he lived in the cemetery. When he saw Jesus he screamed, fell before him, and bellowed, "What business do you have messing with me? You're Jesus, Son of the High God, but don't give me a hard time!" (The man said this because Jesus had started to order the unclean spirit out of him.) Time after time the demon threw the man into convulsions. He had been placed under constant guard and tied with chains and shackles, but crazed and driven wild by the demon, he would shatter the bonds.

30-31 Jesus asked him, "What is your name?"

"Mob. My name is Mob," he said, because many demons afflicted him. And they begged Jesus desperately not to order them to the bottomless pit.

32-33 A large herd of pigs was browsing and rooting on a nearby hill. The demons begged Jesus to order them into the pigs. He gave the order. It was even worse for the pigs than for the man. Crazed, they stampeded over a cliff into the lake and drowned.

34-36 Those tending the pigs, scared to death, bolted and told their story in town and country. People went out to see what had happened. They came to Jesus and found the man from whom the demons had been sent, sitting there at Jesus' feet, wearing decent clothes and making sense. It was a holy moment, and for a short time they were more reverent than curious. Then those who had seen it happen told how the demoniac had been saved.

37-39 Later, a great many people from the Gerasene countryside got together and asked Jesus to leave—too much change, too fast, and they were scared. So Jesus got back in the boat and set off. The man whom he had delivered from the demons asked to go with him, but he sent him back, saying, "Go home and tell everything God did in you." So he went back and preached all over town everything Jesus had done in him.

HIS TOUCH

40-42 On his return, Jesus was welcomed by a crowd. They were all there expecting him. A man came up, Jairus by name. He was president of the meeting place. He fell at Jesus' feet and begged him to come to his home because his twelve-year-old daughter, his only child, was dying. Jesus went with him, making his way through the pushing, jostling crowd.

43-45 In the crowd that day there was a woman who for twelve years had been afflicted with hemorrhages. She had spent every penny she had on doctors but not one had been able to help her. She slipped in from behind and touched the edge of Jesus' robe. At that very moment her hemorrhaging stopped. Jesus said, "Who touched me?"

When no one stepped forward, Peter said, "But Master, we've got crowds of people on our hands. Dozens have touched you."

46 Jesus insisted, "Someone touched me. I felt power discharging from me."

47 When the woman realized that she couldn't remain hidden, she knelt trembling before him. In front of all the people, she blurted out her story—why she touched him and how at that same moment she was healed.

48 Jesus said, "Daughter, you took a risk trusting me, and now you're healed and whole. Live well, live blessed!"

49 While he was still talking, someone from the leader's house came up and told him, "Your daughter died. No need now to bother the Teacher."

50-51 Jesus overheard and said, "Don't be upset. Just trust me and everything will be all right." Going into the house, he wouldn't let anyone enter with him except Peter, John, James, and the child's parents.

52-53 Everyone was crying and carrying on over her. Jesus said, "Don't cry. She didn't die; she's sleeping." They laughed at him. They knew she was dead.

54-56 Then Jesus, gripping her hand, called, "My dear child, get up." She was up in an instant, up and breathing again! He told them to give her something to eat. Her parents were ecstatic, but Jesus warned them to keep quiet. "Don't tell a soul what happened in this room."

ΔΔΔ

S.O.A.P.

BIBLE STUDY METHOD

We first encountered S.O.A.P. (which stand for Study, Observe, Apply, and Pray) in Luke 1. Remember, it's a simple method of Bible Study that you can use for any passage of scripture.

1. Study

Study the scripture. You've already done this, but consider taking the time to reread Luke 8. Ask the Holy Spirit to illuminate what He would like you to see. Highlight words or phrases that stand out to you.

2. Observe

Make some observations. Who is this passage written by? To whom is this written to? Is there anything in this passage I've never noticed before? What is the context of this passage? (In other words, what comes before and after these verses)? Are there any specific words or phrases that stand out to me? Does this passage remind me of any other Bible passages?

3. Apply

For this step, ask yourself one simple question, "What is the Holy Spirit saying to me through these verses?" Take a moment to quiet yourself, and listen for God's voice. He may have something to say regarding your thoughts, your actions, your relationships, your plans, your dreams — and unless we consciously take the time to just listen, we may miss out on what he has to say.

4. Pray

Your prayer could include things like: thanking God for the truths that He highlighted during your study of the the Bible today, thanking him for what he helped you to observe, and asking for his help to apply these truths and observations to your life.

KEEP TRUSTING IN JESUS

DEVOTIONAL READING

March 31 reading of bibleinoneyear.org by Nicky Gumbel

"...he said to his disciples, "Why can't you trust
me?" (Luke 8:25, The Message)

There may be times in your life when fear seems overwhelming. Sometimes it comes like the unexpected storm that the disciples experienced (vv.22–25).

This section starts with an extraordinary combination of intimacy and awe. Jesus says of his followers that 'those who hear God's word and put it into practice' (v.21) will have an intimate relationship with him. They are his 'mother and brothers' (v.21).

Intimacy and 'fear' (in the good sense) are not opposites – they complement one another. This is true of the best relationships – whether in marriage, in close friendships or with parents and children. Extraordinary intimacy is combined with healthy respect.

The disciples experienced two different types of fear when they were on the lake with Jesus. When a storm came, they were in 'great danger' (v.23) and the disciples were afraid. They woke Jesus and said, 'Master, Master, we're going to drown!' (v.24a).

Jesus 'got up and rebuked the wind and the raging waters; the storm subsided, and all was calm' (v.24b). He said to his disciples, 'Where is your faith?' (v.25a). Again, we see the contrast between unhealthy fear and faith. Jesus said to them, 'Why can't you trust me?' (v.25a, MSG).

The answer to their fear is so simple and yet so hard to put into practice. I have found it is a lesson I have had to keep re-learning. In the midst of your fears, keep trusting Jesus – keep putting your confidence in him. Sometimes Jesus calms the storm as he did here. Sometimes he lets the storm rage and he calms you.

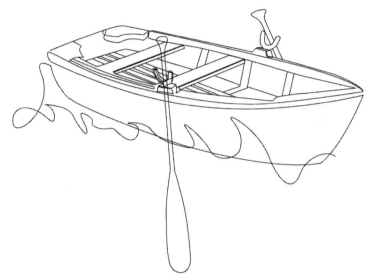

The disciples' response to Jesus is one of healthy fear – absolute awe (v.25b, MSG), amazement and humility in the presence of Jesus. They ask each other: 'Who is this?' (v.25).

Their question is answered by the demon-possessed man whom Jesus heals. Jesus is the 'Son of the Most High God' (v.28).

When those tending the pigs saw the man healed, 'sitting at Jesus' feet, dressed and in his right mind', they 'were afraid' (v.35) – 'scared to death' (v.34, MSG). They asked Jesus to leave because they were 'overcome with fear' (v.37) – 'too much change, too fast and they were scared' (v.37, MSG).

This was again the wrong kind of fear. They were afraid because they had lost valuable pigs. What would it be next? They could not see the immense value of one person's life. They rejected Jesus out of fear, but Jesus had no fear of them or anything else.

Jesus had an interesting approach to follow-up. The man who had been demon-possessed wanted 'to go with him' (v.38). However, Jesus' approach is to get him involved in telling others straight away. He says, '"Return home and tell how much God has done for you." So the man went away and told all over the town how much Jesus had done for him' (v.39).

In encountering Jesus, he had encountered God. Luke interchanges, 'how much *God* has done for you' (v.39a) and 'how much *Jesus* had done for him' (v.39b). Jesus is God. This is why ultimately Jesus is the answer to all our unhealthy fears. Don't be overcome by fear but overcome your fear with Jesus.

> Lord, give me a healthy fear – awe, amazement and
> humility in the presence of Jesus and a faith in him that
> delivers me from all my unhealthy fears.

LUKE 9

"Who do you say I am?"

LUKE 9 (NIV)

New International Version

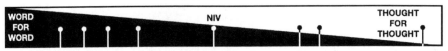

JESUS SENDS OUT THE TWELVE

When Jesus had called the Twelve together, he gave them power and authority to drive out all demons and to cure diseases,

2 and he sent them out to proclaim the kingdom of God and to heal the sick.

3 He told them: "Take nothing for the journey—no staff, no bag, no bread, no money, no extra shirt.

4 Whatever house you enter, stay there until you leave that town.

5 If people do not welcome you, leave their town and shake the dust off your feet as a testimony against them."

6 So they set out and went from village to village, proclaiming the good news and healing people everywhere.

7 Now Herod the tetrarch heard about all that was going on. And he was perplexed because some were saying that John had been raised from the dead,

8 others that Elijah had appeared, and still others that one of the prophets of long ago had come back to life.

9 But Herod said, "I beheaded John. Who, then, is this I hear such things about?" And he tried to see him.

JESUS FEEDS THE FIVE THOUSAND

10 When the apostles returned, they reported to Jesus what they had done. Then he took them with him and they withdrew by themselves to a town called Bethsaida,

11 but the crowds learned about it and followed him. He welcomed them and spoke to them about the kingdom of God, and healed those who needed healing.

12 Late in the afternoon the Twelve came to him and said, "Send the crowd away so they can go to the surrounding villages and countryside and find food and lodging, because we are in a remote place here."

13 He replied, "You give them something to eat." They answered, "We have only five loaves of bread and two fish—unless we go and buy food for all this crowd."

14 (About five thousand men were there.) But he said to his disciples, "Have them sit down in groups of about fifty each."

15 The disciples did so, and everyone sat down.

16 Taking the five loaves and the two fish and looking up to heaven, he gave thanks and broke them. Then he gave them to the disciples to distribute to the people.

17 They all ate and were satisfied, and the disciples picked up twelve basketfuls of broken pieces that were left over.

PETER DECLARES THAT JESUS IS THE MESSIAH

18 Once when Jesus was praying in private and his disciples were with him, he asked them, "Who do the crowds say I am?"

19 They replied, "Some say John the Baptist; others say Elijah; and still others, that one of the prophets of long ago has come back to life."

20 "But what about you?" he asked. "Who do you say I am?" Peter answered, "God's Messiah."

JESUS PREDICTS HIS DEATH

21 Jesus strictly warned them not to tell this to anyone.

22 And he said, "The Son of Man must suffer many things and be rejected by the elders, the chief priests and the teachers of the law, and he must be killed and on the third day be raised to life."

23 Then he said to them all: "Whoever wants to be my disciple must deny themselves and take up their cross daily and follow me.

24 For whoever wants to save their life will lose it, but whoever loses their life for me will save it.

25 What good is it for someone to gain the whole world, and yet lose or forfeit their very self?

26 Whoever is ashamed of me and my words, the Son of Man will be ashamed of them when he comes in his glory and in the glory of the Father and of the holy angels.

27 "Truly I tell you, some who are standing here will not taste death before they see the kingdom of God."

THE TRANSFIGURATION

28 About eight days after Jesus said this, he took Peter, John and James with him and went up onto a mountain to pray.

29 As he was praying, the appearance of his face changed, and his clothes became as bright as a flash of lightning.

30 Two men, Moses and Elijah, appeared in glorious splendor, talking with Jesus.

31 They spoke about his departure, which he was about to bring to fulfillment at Jerusalem.

32 Peter and his companions were very sleepy, but when they became fully awake, they saw his glory and the two men standing with him.

33 As the men were leaving Jesus, Peter said to him, "Master, it is good for us to be here. Let us put up three shelters—one for you, one for Moses and one for Elijah." (He did not know what he was saying.)

34 While he was speaking, a cloud appeared and covered them, and they were afraid as they entered the cloud.

35 A voice came from the cloud, saying, "This is my Son, whom I have chosen; listen to him."

36 When the voice had spoken, they found that Jesus was alone. The disciples kept this to themselves and did not tell anyone at that time what they had seen.

JESUS HEALS A DEMON-POSSESSED BOY

37 The next day, when they came down from the mountain, a large crowd met him.

38 A man in the crowd called out, "Teacher, I beg you to look at my son, for he is my only child.

39 A spirit seizes him and he suddenly screams; it throws him into convulsions so that he foams at the mouth. It scarcely ever leaves him and is destroying him.

40 I begged your disciples to drive it out, but they could not."

41 "You unbelieving and perverse generation," Jesus replied, "how long shall I stay with you and put up with you? Bring your son here."

42 Even while the boy was coming, the demon threw him to the ground in a convulsion. But Jesus rebuked the impure spirit, healed the boy and gave him back to his father.

43 And they were all amazed at the greatness of God. While everyone was marveling at all that Jesus did, he said to his disciples,

JESUS PREDICTS HIS DEATH A SECOND TIME

44 "Listen carefully to what I am about to tell you: The Son of Man is going to be delivered into the hands of men."

45 But they did not understand what this meant. It was hidden from them, so that they did not grasp it, and they were afraid to ask him about it.

46 An argument started among the disciples as to which of them would be the greatest.

47 Jesus, knowing their thoughts, took a little child and had him stand beside him.

48 Then he said to them, "Whoever welcomes this little child in my name welcomes me; and whoever welcomes me welcomes the one who sent me. For it is the one who is least among you all who is the greatest."

49 "Master," said John, "we saw someone driving out demons in your name and we tried to stop him, because he is not one of us."

50 "Do not stop him," Jesus said, "for whoever is not against you is for you."

SAMARITAN OPPOSITION

51 As the time approached for him to be taken up to heaven, Jesus resolutely set out for Jerusalem.

52 And he sent messengers on ahead, who went into a Samaritan village to get things ready for him;

53 but the people there did not welcome him, because he was heading for Jerusalem.

54 When the disciples James and John saw this, they asked, "Lord, do you want us to call fire down from heaven to destroy them?"

55 But Jesus turned and rebuked them.

56 Then he and his disciples went to another village.

THE COST OF FOLLOWING JESUS

57 As they were walking along the road, a man said to him, "I will follow you wherever you go."

58 Jesus replied, "Foxes have dens and birds have nests, but the Son of Man has no place to lay his head."

59 He said to another man, "Follow me." But he replied, "Lord, first let me go and bury my father."

60 Jesus said to him, "Let the dead bury their own dead, but you go and proclaim the kingdom of God."

61 Still another said, "I will follow you, Lord; but first let me go back and say goodbye to my family."

62 Jesus replied, "No one who puts a hand to the plow and looks back is fit for service in the kingdom of God."

ΔΔΔ

R.E.A.P.

BIBLE STUDY METHOD

We first encountered R.E.A.P. (which stand for Read, Examine, Apply, and Pray) in Luke 2. Here's a reminder of how it works:

1. Read

You've already done this, but consider taking the time to *reread* Luke 9. Ask the Holy Spirit to illuminate what He would like you to see. Highlight words or phrases that stand out to you.

2. Examine

Ask yourself a few questions, such as: What is going on in the passage? What are the circumstances? Who are the main characters? What are the major themes? What is the context of this passage? (In other words, what comes before and after these verses)? Are there any specific words or phrases that stand out to me? Does this passage remind me of any other Bible passages?

3. Apply

Here's a few simple questions you can ask to help you apply Luke 9 (and any) passage: Is there a truth to believe? A sin to repent of? A promise to claim? A command to follow? What are things that need to change in light of this text? How will I live differently and be different because of what I just read? What is the Holy Spirit saying to me through these verses?

4. Pray

Your prayer could include things like: thanking God for the truths that He highlighted in your reading, thanking him for what he helped you to examine, and asking for his help to apply these to your life.

"YES—BUT...!"

DEVOTIONAL READING

May 30 reading of Oswald Chambers, My Utmost for His Highest: Selections for the Year (Grand Rapids, MI: Oswald Chambers Publications; Marshall Pickering, 1986).

"I will follow you, Lord; but..." (Luke 9:61, NIV)

Supposing God tells you to do something which is an enormous test to your common sense, what are you going to do? Hang back? If you get into the habit of doing a thing in the physical domain, you will do it every time until you break the habit determinedly; and the same is true spiritually. Again and again you will get up to what Jesus Christ wants, and every time you will turn back when it comes to the point, until you abandon resolutely.

'Yes, but—supposing I do obey God in this matter, what about ...?'

'Yes, I will obey God if He will let me use my common sense, but don't ask me to take a step in the dark.'

Jesus Christ demands of the man who trusts Him the same reckless sporting spirit that the natural man exhibits. If a man is going to do anything worth while, there are times when he has to risk everything on his leap, and in the spiritual domain Jesus Christ demands that you risk everything you hold by common sense and leap into what He says, and immediately you do, you find that what He says fits on as solidly as common sense.

At the bar of *common sense* Jesus Christ's statements may seem mad; but bring them to the bar of *faith*, and you begin to find with awestruck spirit that they are the words of God.

Trust entirely in God, and when He brings you to the venture, see that you take it.

We act like pagans in a crisis, only one out of a crowd is daring enough to bank his faith in the character of God.

LUKE 10

*"Blessed are the eyes which see
the things that ye see"*

LUKE 10 (KJV)

King James Version

MISSION OF THE SEVENTY

After these things the Lord appointed other seventy also, and sent them two and two before his face into every city and place, whither he himself would come.

2 Therefore said he unto them, The harvest truly is great, but the labourers are few: pray ye therefore the Lord of the harvest, that he would send forth labourers into his harvest.

3 Go your ways: behold, I send you forth as lambs among wolves.

4 Carry neither purse, nor scrip, nor shoes: and salute no man by the way.

5 And into whatsoever house ye enter, first say, Peace be to this house.

6 And if the son of peace be there, your peace shall rest upon it: if not, it shall turn to you again.

7 And in the same house remain, eating and drinking such things as they give: for the labourer is worthy of his hire. Go not from house to house.

8 And into whatsoever city ye enter, and they receive you, eat such things as are set before you:

9 And heal the sick that are therein, and say unto them, The kingdom of God is come nigh unto you.

10 But into whatsoever city ye enter, and they receive you not, go your ways out into the streets of the same, and say,

11 Even the very dust of your city, which cleaveth on us, we do wipe off against you: notwithstanding be ye sure of this, that the kingdom of God is come nigh unto you.

12 But I say unto you, that it shall be more tolerable in that day for Sodom, than for that city.

13 Woe unto thee, Chorazin! woe unto thee, Bethsaida! for if the mighty works had been done in Tyre and Sidon, which have been done in you, they had a great while ago repented, sitting in sackcloth and ashes.

14 But it shall be more tolerable for Tyre and Sidon at the judgment, than for you.

15 And thou, Capernaum, which art exalted to heaven, shalt be thrust down to hell.

16 He that heareth you heareth me; and he that despiseth you despiseth me; and he that despiseth me despiseth him that sent me.

RETURN OF THE SEVENTY

17 And the seventy returned again with joy, saying, Lord, even the devils are subject unto us through thy name.

18 And he said unto them, I beheld Satan as lightning fall from heaven.

19 Behold, I give unto you power to tread on serpents and scorpions, and over all the power of the enemy: and nothing shall by any means hurt you.

20 Notwithstanding in this rejoice not, that the spirits are subject unto you; but rather rejoice, because your names are written in heaven.

21 In that hour Jesus rejoiced in spirit, and said, I thank thee, O Father, Lord of heaven and earth, that thou hast hid these things from the wise and prudent, and hast revealed them unto babes: even so, Father; for so it seemed good in thy sight.

22 All things are delivered to me of my Father: and no man knoweth who the Son is, but the Father; and who the Father is, but the Son, and he to whom the Son will reveal him.

23 And he turned him unto his disciples, and said privately, Blessed are the eyes which see the things that ye see:

24 For I tell you, that many prophets and kings have desired to see those things which ye see, and have not seen them; and to hear those things which ye hear, and have not heard them.

HOW TO INHERIT ETERNAL LIFE

25 And, behold, a certain lawyer stood up, and tempted him, saying, Master, what shall I do to inherit eternal life?

26 He said unto him, What is written in the law? how readest thou?

27 And he answering said, Thou shalt love the Lord thy God with all thy heart, and with all thy soul, and with all thy strength, and with all thy mind; and thy neighbour as thyself.

28 And he said unto him, Thou hast answered right: this do, and thou shalt live.

PARABLE OF THE GOOD SAMARITAN

29 But he, willing to justify himself, said unto Jesus, And who is my neighbour?

30 And Jesus answering said, A certain man went down from Jerusalem to Jericho, and fell among thieves, which stripped him of his raiment, and wounded him, and departed, leaving him half dead.

31 And by chance there came down a certain priest that way: and when he saw him, he passed by on the other side.

32 And likewise a Levite, when he was at the place, came and looked on him, and passed by on the other side.

33 But a certain Samaritan, as he journeyed, came where he was: and when he saw him, he had compassion on him,

34 And went to him, and bound up his wounds, pouring in oil and wine, and set him on his own beast, and brought him to an inn, and took care of him.

35 And on the morrow when he departed, he took out two pence, and gave them to the host, and said unto him, Take care of him; and whatsoever thou spendest more, when I come again, I will repay thee.

36 Which now of these three, thinkest thou, was neighbour unto him that fell among the thieves?

37 And he said, He that shewed mercy on him. Then said Jesus unto him, Go, and do thou likewise.

MARY AND MARTHA ARE CONTRASTED

38 Now it came to pass, as they went, that he entered into a certain village: and a certain woman named Martha received him into her house.

39 And she had a sister called Mary, which also sat at Jesus' feet, and heard his word.

40 But Martha was cumbered about much serving, and came to him, and said, Lord, dost thou not care that my sister hath left me to serve alone? bid her therefore that she help me.

41 And Jesus answered and said unto her, Martha, Martha, thou art careful and troubled about many things:

42 But one thing is needful: and Mary hath chosen that good part, which shall not be taken away from her.

ΔΔΔ

4R'S

BIBLE STUDY METHOD

*The four R's: Read, Reflect, Respond, and Rest are back again.
Remember? We looked at them in chapter 3. Let's dig in!*

1. Read

You've already done this, but consider taking the time to *reread* Luke 10. Ask the Holy Spirit to illuminate what He would like you to see. Highlight words or phrases that stand out to you.

2. Reflect

What is Luke 10 saying to you? What did you hear, or what are you feeling or thinking? Consider asking a few of the questions we used in S.O.A.P and R.E.A.P, such as: what is the context of Luke 10? Are there any specific words or phrases that stand out? Does this passage remind me of any other Bible passages?

3. Respond

What is your response to Luke 10? Ask yourself one simple question, "What is the Holy Spirit saying to me through these verses?" Take a moment to quiet yourself, and listen for God's voice. He may have something to say regarding your thoughts, your actions, your relationships, your plans, and your dreams.

4. Rest

Quietly ponder what you've read, and how you've chosen to respond—trusting God for the strength and courage necessary.

SERVICE TO AND COMMUNION WITH JESUS

DEVOTIONAL READING

January 24 reading of C. H. Spurgeon, Morning and Evening: Daily Readings (London: Passmore & Alabaster, 1896).

"...Martha was cumbered about much serving..." (Luke 10:40, KJV)

Her fault was not that she served: the condition of a servant well becomes every Christian. "I serve," should be the motto of all the princes of the royal family of heaven.

Nor was it her fault that she had *"much serving."* We cannot do too much. Let us do all that we possibly can; let head, and heart, and hands, be engaged in the Master's service.

It was no fault of hers that she was busy preparing a feast for the Master. Happy Martha, to have an opportunity of entertaining so blessed a guest; and happy, too, to have the spirit to throw her whole soul so heartily into the engagement.

Her fault was that she grew *"cumbered* with much serving," so that she forgot *him*, and only remembered the service. She allowed service to override communion, and so presented one duty stained with the blood of another.

We ought to be Martha and Mary in one: we should do much service, and have much communion at the same time. For this we need great grace. It is easier to serve than to commune.

Joshua never grew weary in fighting with the Amalekites; but Moses, on the top of the mountain in prayer, needed two helpers to sustain his hands. The more spiritual the exercise, the sooner we tire in it. The choicest fruits are the hardest to rear: the most heavenly graces are the most difficult to cultivate.

Beloved, while we do not neglect external things, which are good enough in themselves, we ought also to see to it that we enjoy living, personal fellowship with Jesus. See to it that sitting at the Saviour's feet is not neglected, even though it be under the specious pretext of doing him service.

The first thing for our soul's health, the first thing for his glory, and the first thing for our own usefulness, is to keep ourselves in perpetual communion with the Lord Jesus, and to see that the vital spirituality of our religion is maintained over and above everything else in the world.

ΔΔΔ

LUKE 11

"Lord, teach us to pray"

LUKE 11 (NKJV)

New King James Version

THE LORD'S PRAYER

Now it came to pass, as He was praying in a certain place, when He ceased, that one of His disciples said to Him, "Lord, teach us to pray, as John also taught his disciples."

2 So He said to them, "When you pray, say: Our Father in heaven, Hallowed be Your name. Your kingdom come. Your will be done On earth as it is in heaven.

3 Give us day by day our daily bread.

4 And forgive us our sins, For we also forgive everyone who is indebted to us. And do not lead us into temptation, But deliver us from the evil one."

PARABLE OF THE PERSISTENT FRIEND

5 And He said to them, "Which of you shall have a friend, and go to him at midnight and say to him, 'Friend, lend me three loaves;

6 for a friend of mine has come to me on his journey, and I have nothing to set before him';

7 and he will answer from within and say, 'Do not trouble me; the door is now shut, and my children are with me in bed; I cannot rise and give to you'?

8 I say to you, though he will not rise and give to him because he is his friend, yet because of his persistence he will rise and give him as many as he needs.

9 "So I say to you, ask, and it will be given to you; seek, and you will find; knock, and it will be opened to you.

10 For everyone who asks receives, and he who seeks finds, and to him who knocks it will be opened.

PARABLE OF THE GOOD FATHER

11 If a son asks for bread from any father among you, will he give him a stone? Or if he asks for a fish, will he give him a serpent instead of a fish?

12 Or if he asks for an egg, will he offer him a scorpion?

13 If you then, being evil, know how to give good gifts to your children, how much more will your heavenly Father give the Holy Spirit to those who ask Him!"

CHRIST HEALS THE DEMONIAC

14 And He was casting out a demon, and it was mute. So it was, when the demon had gone out, that the mute spoke; and the multitudes marveled.

CHRIST'S POWER NOT FROM SATAN

15 But some of them said, "He casts out demons by Beelzebub, the ruler of the demons."

16 Others, testing Him, sought from Him a sign from heaven.

17 But He, knowing their thoughts, said to them: "Every kingdom divided against itself is brought to desolation, and a house divided against a house falls.

18 If Satan also is divided against himself, how will his kingdom stand? Because you say I cast out demons by Beelzebub.

19 And if I cast out demons by Beelzebub, by whom do your sons cast them out? Therefore they will be your judges.

20 But if I cast out demons with the finger of God, surely the kingdom of God has come upon you.

21 When a strong man, fully armed, guards his own palace, his goods are in peace.

22 But when a stronger than he comes upon him and overcomes him, he takes from him all his armor in which he trusted, and divides his spoils.

23 He who is not with Me is against Me, and he who does not gather with Me scatters.

24 "When an unclean spirit goes out of a man, he goes through dry places, seeking rest; and finding none, he says, 'I will return to my house from which I came.'

25 And when he comes, he finds it swept and put in order.

26 Then he goes and takes with him seven other spirits more wicked than himself, and they enter and dwell there; and the last state of that man is worse than the first."

27 And it happened, as He spoke these things, that a certain woman from the crowd raised her voice and said to Him, "Blessed is the womb that bore You, and the breasts which nursed You!"

28 But He said, "More than that, blessed are those who hear the word of God and keep it!"

CHRIST'S ONLY SIGN IS JONAH

29 And while the crowds were thickly gathered together, He began to say, "This is an evil generation. It seeks a sign, and no sign will be given to it except the sign of Jonah the prophet.

30 For as Jonah became a sign to the Ninevites, so also the Son of Man will be to this generation.

31 The queen of the South will rise up in the judgment with the men of this generation and condemn them, for she came from the ends of the earth to hear the wisdom of Solomon; and indeed a greater than Solomon is here.

32 The men of Nineveh will rise up in the judgment with this generation and condemn it, for they repented at the preaching of Jonah; and indeed a greater than Jonah is here.

PARABLE OF THE LIGHTED LAMP

33 "No one, when he has lit a lamp, puts it in a secret place or under a basket, but on a lampstand, that those who come in may see the light.

34 The lamp of the body is the eye. Therefore, when your eye is good, your whole body also is full of light. But when your eye is bad, your body also is full of darkness.

35 Therefore take heed that the light which is in you is not darkness.

36 If then your whole body is full of light, having no part dark, the whole body will be full of light, as when the bright shining of a lamp gives you light."

"WOES" ON THE PHARISEES

37 And as He spoke, a certain Pharisee asked Him to dine with him. So He went in and sat down to eat.

38 When the Pharisee saw it, he marveled that He had not first washed before dinner.

39 Then the Lord said to him, "Now you Pharisees make the outside of the cup and dish clean, but your inward part is full of greed and wickedness.

40 Foolish ones! Did not He who made the outside make the inside also?

41 But rather give alms of such things as you have; then indeed all things are clean to you.

42 "But woe to you Pharisees! For you tithe mint and rue and all manner of herbs, and pass by justice and the love of God. These

you ought to have done, without leaving the others undone.

43 Woe to you Pharisees! For you love the best seats in the synagogues and greetings in the marketplaces.

44 Woe to you, scribes and Pharisees, hypocrites! For you are like graves which are not seen, and the men who walk over them are not aware of them."

"WOES" ON THE LAWYERS

45 Then one of the lawyers answered and said to Him, "Teacher, by saying these things You reproach us also."

46 And He said, "Woe to you also, lawyers! For you load men with burdens hard to bear, and you yourselves do not touch the burdens with one of your fingers.

47 Woe to you! For you build the tombs of the prophets, and your fathers killed them.

48 In fact, you bear witness that you approve the deeds of your fathers; for they indeed killed them, and you build their tombs.

49 Therefore the wisdom of God also said, 'I will send them prophets and apostles, and some of them they will kill and persecute,'

50 that the blood of all the prophets which was shed from the foundation of the world may be required of this generation,

51 from the blood of Abel to the blood of Zechariah who perished between the altar and the temple. Yes, I say to you, it shall be required of this generation.

52 "Woe to you lawyers! For you have taken away the key of knowledge. You did not enter in yourselves, and those who were entering in you hindered."

53 And as He said these things to them, the scribes and the Pharisees began to assail Him vehemently, and to cross-examine Him about many things,

54 lying in wait for Him, and seeking to catch Him in something He might say, that they might accuse Him.

ΔΔΔ

C.O.R.E

BIBLE STUDY METHOD

C.O.R.E. is a method I personally created, and I hope you find it useful. (We first looked at it in Luke 4). You may want to consider using it the next time you have an opportunity to teach the Bible.

1. Catalytic Question

Consider taking a moment to reread Luke 11. As you do, see if there is a big question that Luke 11 seems to be answering. This big question is your *Catalytic* Question—the kind of question that sparks additional thoughts.

2. Objective Sentence

The objective sentence is your *answer* to the catalytic question, which is based on what you just read in Luke 11. For example, if your catalytic question is, "What did Jesus teach us to include in our prayers?" Your objective sentence might say, "Jesus taught us to include at least 3 elements."

3. Rationale

The Rationale is where you provide more details to the objective sentence. Our rationale for, "Jesus taught us to include at least 3 elements" could be something like: 1) Worship (hallowed be Your name), 2) Faith (Your kingdom come. Your will be done), and 3) A Clean Heart (forgive us our sins).

4. Express Thanks

Take a moment to express thanks to God for what he has shown you in his Word today.

CRANBERRY BAGELS

DEVOTIONAL READING

Day 67 reading of John Baker and Johnny Baker, Celebrate Recovery Daily Devotional: 366 Devotionals (Grand Rapids, MI: Zondervan, 2013).

"So I say to you, ask, and it will be given to you; seek, and you will find; knock, and it will be opened to you. For everyone who asks receives, and he who seeks finds, and to him who knocks it will be opened. (Luke 11:9-11, NKJV)

Once we enter into relationship with God, the Bible tells us that he becomes our heavenly Father, and he invites us to come to him any time with our requests. But sometimes because of our past mistakes, we feel we should not ask him for anything—at least nothing too small or insignificant—until we've proven ourselves.

Of course, God answers our prayers in accordance with his own goodness, not ours, and he loves us despite our mistakes. I saw this principle at work a few weeks ago. On visits to see our kids, I have made it my habit to go out early in the morning, while everyone else is asleep, and pick up cranberry bagels. But on a recent visit, I had not yet done that. On the evening of the fourth day, I was saying goodnight prayers with my two-year-old grandson. "Please help Papa get some bagels," he prayed. I hadn't realize how important this tradition had become to him.

Guess what was waiting for him the next morning? That's right, warm fresh bagels. It didn't matter how my grandson had acted since we'd arrived. He asked, and I responded.

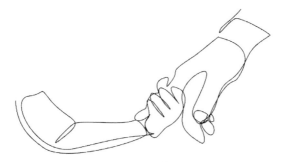

Our Father God is waiting to hear from us—from the biggest request to the smallest. When we reach out to him, he is always listening.

Father, thank you for always hearing my prayers. I'm so grateful for your love and your care. In Jesus' name, Amen.

LUKE 12

"Keep your lamps burning"

LUKE 12 (ESV)

English Standard Version

BEWARE OF THE LEAVEN OF THE PHARISEES

In the meantime, when so many thousands of the people had gathered together that they were trampling one another, he began to say to his disciples first, "Beware of the leaven of the Pharisees, which is hypocrisy.

2 Nothing is covered up that will not be revealed, or hidden that will not be known.

3 Therefore whatever you have said in the dark shall be heard in the light, and what you have whispered in private rooms shall be proclaimed on the housetops.

HAVE NO FEAR

4 "I tell you, my friends, do not fear those who kill the body, and after that have nothing more that they can do.

5 But I will warn you whom to fear: fear him who, after he has killed, has authority to cast into hell. Yes, I tell you, fear him!

6 Are not five sparrows sold for two pennies? And not one of them is forgotten before God.

7 Why, even the hairs of your head are all numbered. Fear not; you are of more value than many sparrows.

ACKNOWLEDGE CHRIST BEFORE MEN

8 "And I tell you, everyone who acknowledges me before men,

the Son of Man also will acknowledge before the angels of God,

9 but the one who denies me before men will be denied before the angels of God.

10 And everyone who speaks a word against the Son of Man will be forgiven, but the one who blasphemes against the Holy Spirit will not be forgiven.

11 And when they bring you before the synagogues and the rulers and the authorities, do not be anxious about how you should defend yourself or what you should say,

12 for the Holy Spirit will teach you in that very hour what you ought to say."

THE PARABLE OF THE RICH FOOL

13 Someone in the crowd said to him, "Teacher, tell my brother to divide the inheritance with me."

14 But he said to him, "Man, who made me a judge or arbitrator over you?"

15 And he said to them, "Take care, and be on your guard against all covetousness, for one's life does not consist in the abundance of his possessions."

16 And he told them a parable, saying, "The land of a rich man produced plentifully,

17 and he thought to himself, 'What shall I do, for I have nowhere to store my crops?'

18 And he said, 'I will do this: I will tear down my barns and build larger ones, and there I will store all my grain and my goods.

19 And I will say to my soul, "Soul, you have ample goods laid up for many years; relax, eat, drink, be merry." '

20 But God said to him, 'Fool! This night your soul is required of you, and the things you have prepared, whose will they be?'

21 So is the one who lays up treasure for himself and is not rich toward God."

DO NOT BE ANXIOUS

22 And he said to his disciples, "Therefore I tell you, do not be anxious about your life, what you will eat, nor about your body, what you will put on.

23 For life is more than food, and the body more than clothing.

24 Consider the ravens: they neither sow nor reap, they have neither storehouse nor barn, and yet God feeds them. Of how much more value are you than the birds!

25 And which of you by being anxious can add a single hour to his span of life?

26 If then you are not able to do as small a thing as that, why are you anxious about the rest?

27 Consider the lilies, how they grow: they neither toil nor spin, yet I tell you, even Solomon in all his glory was not arrayed like one of these.

28 But if God so clothes the grass, which is alive in the field today, and tomorrow is thrown into the oven, how much more will he clothe you, O you of little faith!

29 And do not seek what you are to eat and what you are to drink, nor be worried.

30 For all the nations of the world seek after these things, and your Father knows that you need them.

31 Instead, seek his kingdom, and these things will be added to you.

32 "Fear not, little flock, for it is your Father's good pleasure to give you the kingdom.

33 Sell your possessions, and give to the needy. Provide yourselves with moneybags that do not grow old, with a treasure in the heavens that does not fail, where no thief approaches and no moth destroys.

34 For where your treasure is, there will your heart be also.

YOU MUST BE READY

35 "Stay dressed for action and keep your lamps burning,

36 and be like men who are waiting for their master to come home from the wedding feast, so that they may open the door to him at once when he comes and knocks.

37 Blessed are those servants whom the master finds awake when he comes. Truly, I say to you, he will dress himself for service and have them recline at table, and he will come and serve them.

38 If he comes in the second watch, or in the third, and finds them awake, blessed are those servants!

39 But know this, that if the master of the house had known at what hour the thief was coming, he would not have left his house to be broken into.

40 You also must be ready, for the Son of Man is coming at an hour you do not expect."

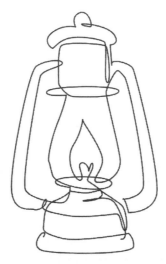

41 Peter said, "Lord, are you telling this parable for us or for all?"

42 And the Lord said, "Who then is the faithful and wise manager, whom his master will set over his household, to give them their portion of food at the proper time?

43 Blessed is that servant whom his master will find so doing when he comes.

44 Truly, I say to you, he will set him over all his possessions.

45 But if that servant says to himself, 'My master is delayed in coming,' and begins to beat the male and female servants, and to eat and drink and get drunk,

46 the master of that servant will come on a day when he does not expect him and at an hour he does not know, and will cut him in pieces and put him with the unfaithful.

47 And that servant who knew his master's will but did not get ready or act according to his will, will receive a severe beating.

48 But the one who did not know, and did what deserved a beating, will receive a light beating. Everyone to whom much was given, of him much will be required, and from him to whom they entrusted much, they will demand the more.

NOT PEACE, BUT DIVISION

49 "I came to cast fire on the earth, and would that it were already kindled!

50 I have a baptism to be baptized with, and how great is my distress until it is accomplished!

51 Do you think that I have come to give peace on earth? No, I tell you, but rather division.

52 For from now on in one house there will be five divided, three against two and two against three.

53 They will be divided, father against son and son against father, mother against daughter and daughter against mother, mother-in-law against her daughter-in-law and daughter-in-law against mother-in-law."

54 He also said to the crowds, "When you see a cloud rising in the west, you say at once, 'A shower is coming.' And so it happens.

55 And when you see the south wind blowing, you say, 'There will be scorching heat,' and it happens.

56 You hypocrites! You know how to interpret the appearance of earth and sky, but why do you not know how to interpret the present time?

SETTLE WITH YOUR ACCUSER

57 "And why do you not judge for yourselves what is right?

58 As you go with your accuser before the magistrate, make an effort to settle with him on the way, lest he drag you to the judge,

and the judge hand you over to the officer, and the officer put you in prison.

59 I tell you, you will never get out until you have paid the very last penny."

ΔΔΔ

DISCOVERY

BIBLE STUDY METHOD

We discovered the Discovery Bible Study (DBS) method back in Luke 5. You may recall that DBS is question-based Bible study that encourages the discovery of the Bible, obeying what is learned, and then sharing it with others.

Read

Begin by reading (and rereading) Luke 12, and then answer the following questions.

Questions

1. What does Luke 12 tell me about God and/or His plan?

2. What does Luke 12 tell me about people?

3. If Luke 12 is truly from God, how will I apply and obey it? (Begin your answer by saying, "I will...")

4. Who needs to hear Luke 12, and when will I share it?

RESTING IN HIS LOVE

DEVOTIONAL READING

January 25 reading of Hannah Whitall Smith and Melvin Easterday Dieter, The Christian's Secret of a Holy Life: The Unpublished Personal Writings of Hannah Whitall Smith (Oak Harbor: Logos Research Systems, Inc., 1997).

For all the nations of the world seek after these things, and your Father knows that you need them. Instead, seek his kingdom, and these things will be added to you. (Luke 12:30-31, ESV)

The Lord has been and is teaching us what a precious thing it is to trust our temporal affairs into His Hands. We have learned Mark 6:33–44 and Luke 12:22–32 are really true for us. It is wonderful that the Lord blesses His children like this, but He Himself has declared it, and His word stands sure.

And oh! it is infinitely precious to trust everything to Him. Even perplexities and trials that drive us to this entire dependence have something very sweet in them, and though often trying to the flesh—still I can thank and bless the Lord for such gracious dealings with me. I am His child—this comprises the whole breadth and extent of my faith. I know that I am "of more value than many sparrows."

Once it was as if I were walking along a certain pathway, upheld and guided it is true by the hand of God, but still walking as we sometimes have seen pictures of children with their guardian angels. I felt that if God should let go of my hand, though I would certainly fall, still I would not fall far, nor be seriously injured.

But now I think far differently. I see God moving swiftly through the awful infinitudes of space and time. I see His arms outstretched over the fearful depths of infinity and eternity, and I see myself lying in those arms—a poor, weak, trembling, sin-defiled thing. I know that the depths are just beneath me and that nothing separates me from them but the arms of mercy in which I am lying; but my upturned face knows nothing but the tender Voice saying "I will never leave thee nor forsake thee."

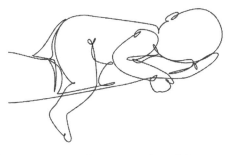

If those arms of mercy should grow weary of carrying me, then I should be lost indeed for I should sink down, down, down into the blackness of darkness forever. But as I lie in their strong embrace, I do not fear this. And the more I see of my own helplessness, and the more I know of my own vileness, the more closely I cling to those Arms of mercy and the more earnestly I gaze into that face of love.

And I say to myself, "He knew all my unworthiness when He loved me and took me into His embrace, and though He continues to know it, He will not cease to love me or cast me off." I rest, oh, I rest in His Love! —Journal, December 4, 1859

ΔΔΔ

LUKE 13

"Enter through the narrow door"

LUKE 13 (CSB)

Christian Standard Bible

REPENT OR PERISH

A t that time, some people came and reported to him about the Galileans whose blood Pilate had mixed with their sacrifices.

2 And he responded to them, "Do you think that these Galileans were more sinful than all the other Galileans because they suffered these things?

3 No, I tell you; but unless you repent, you will all perish as well.

4 Or those eighteen that the tower in Siloam fell on and killed —do you think they were more sinful than all the other people who live in Jerusalem?

5 No, I tell you; but unless you repent, you will all perish as well."

THE PARABLE OF THE BARREN FIG TREE

6 And he told this parable: "A man had a fig tree that was planted in his vineyard. He came looking for fruit on it and found none.

7 He told the vineyard worker, 'Listen, for three years I have come looking for fruit on this fig tree and haven't found any. Cut it down! Why should it even waste the soil?'

8 "But he replied to him, 'Sir, leave it this year also, until I dig around it and fertilize it.

9 Perhaps it will produce fruit next year, but if not, you can cut it down.' "

HEALING A DAUGHTER OF ABRAHAM

10 As he was teaching in one of the synagogues on the Sabbath,

11 a woman was there who had been disabled by a spirit for over eighteen years. She was bent over and could not straighten up at all.

12 When Jesus saw her, he called out to her, "Woman, you are free of your disability."

13 Then he laid his hands on her, and instantly she was restored and began to glorify God.

14 But the leader of the synagogue, indignant because Jesus had healed on the Sabbath, responded by telling the crowd, "There are six days when work should be done; therefore come on those days and be healed and not on the Sabbath day."

15 But the Lord answered him and said, "Hypocrites! Doesn't each one of you untie his ox or donkey from the feeding trough on the Sabbath and lead it to water?

16 Satan has bound this woman, a daughter of Abraham, for eighteen years—shouldn't she be untied from this bondage on the Sabbath day?"

17 When he had said these things, all his adversaries were humiliated, but the whole crowd was rejoicing over all the glorious things he was doing.

THE PARABLES OF THE MUSTARD SEED AND OF THE YEAST

18 He said, therefore, "What is the kingdom of God like, and what can I compare it to?

19 It's like a mustard seed that a man took and sowed in his garden. It grew and became a tree, and the birds of the sky nested in its branches."

20 Again he said, "What can I compare the kingdom of God to?

21 It's like leaven that a woman took and mixed into fifty pounds of flour until all of it was leavened."

THE NARROW WAY

22 He went through one town and village after another, teaching and making his way to Jerusalem.

23 "Lord," someone asked him, "are only a few people going to be saved?" He said to them,

24 "Make every effort to enter through the narrow door, because I tell you, many will try to enter and won't be able

25 once the homeowner gets up and shuts the door. Then you will stand outside and knock on the door, saying, 'Lord, open up for us!' He will answer you, 'I don't know you or where you're from.'

26 Then you will say, 'We ate and drank in your presence, and you taught in our streets.'

27 But he will say, 'I tell you, I don't know you or where you're from. Get away from me, all you evildoers!'

28 There will be weeping and gnashing of teeth in that place, when you see Abraham, Isaac, Jacob, and all the prophets in the kingdom of God, but yourselves thrown out.

29 They will come from east and west, from north and south, to share the banquet in the kingdom of God.

30 Note this: Some who are last will be first, and some who are first will be last."

JESUS AND HEROD ANTIPAS

31 At that time some Pharisees came and told him, "Go, get out of here. Herod wants to kill you."

32 He said to them, "Go tell that fox, 'Look, I'm driving out demons and performing healings today and tomorrow, and on the third day I will complete my work.'

33 Yet it is necessary that I travel today, tomorrow, and the next day, because it is not possible for a prophet to perish outside of Jerusalem.

JESUS' LAMENTATION OVER JERUSALEM

34 "Jerusalem, Jerusalem, who kills the prophets and stones those who are sent to her. How often I wanted to gather your children together, as a hen gathers her chicks under her wings, but you were not willing!

35 See, your house is abandoned to you. I tell you, you will not see me until the time comes when you say, 'Blessed is he who comes in the name of the Lord'!"

C.U.B.E.

BIBLE STUDY METHOD

Time to get our your pens and pencils again! We looked at the C.U.B.E. method back in Luke 6. The letters of C.U.B.E. stands for Circle, Underline, Bracket, and Express.

(Circle)

Read Luke 13 again (out loud) but this time look for anything that has to do with God (Father, Son, or Holy Spirit). Put a (circle) around every mention of his name, including pronouns referring to him.

Underline

Read Luke 13 another time, but this time around, look for statements that talk about how a follower of Jesus *should live*. When you find such a statement, underline it.

[Bracket]

Read Luke 13 once more, but this time look for statements that talk about how a believer should *not* live. When you encounter such a statement, put a set of [brackets] around it.

Express

Congratulations! You have just read the same passage of

scripture 4 times. By circling, underlining, and bracketing you have involved 3 of your senses: sight, sound, and touch. Take a moment to express your worship and gratitude to God for anything he has revealed to you during your study.

RESCUE THE PERISHING

DEVOTIONAL READING

October 2 reading of Kenneth W. Osbeck, Amazing Grace: 366 Inspiring Hymn Stories for Daily Devotions (Grand Rapids, MI: Kregel Publications, 1996), 297.

"No, I tell you; but unless you repent, you will all
perish as well."" (Luke 13:5, CSB)

One of the most tragic words in our vocabulary is the word perishing. Yet it was a word that Jesus Himself often used to describe people who are spiritually alienated from God.

Fanny Crosby (1820–1915), often called the "queen of gospel music," recalled how she wrote this challenging hymn: "I remember writing that hymn in the year 1869. Like many of my hymns, it was written following a personal experience at the New York City Bowery Mission. I usually tried to get to the mission at least one night a week to talk to "my boys." I was addressing a large company of working men one hot summer evening, when the thought kept forcing itself on my mind that some mother's boy must be rescued that night or he might be eternally lost. So I made a pressing plea that if there was a boy present who had wandered from his mother's home and teaching, he should come to me at the end of the service. A young man of 18 came forward—"

"Did you mean me, Miss Crosby? I promised my mother to meet her in heaven, but as I am now living, that will be impossible."

"We prayed for him and suddenly he arose with a new light in his eyes—"

"Now I am ready to meet my mother in heaven, for I have found God."

A few days before, William Doane, composer of the music, had sent Fanny Crosby a tune for a new song to be titled "Rescue the Perishing." It was to be based on the text "Go out into the highways and hedges, and compel them to come in, that my house may be filled" (Luke 14:23).

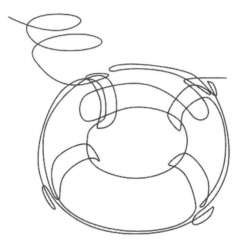

Rescue the perishing, care for the dying, snatch them in
pity from sin and the grave; weep o'er the erring one, lift
up the fallen, tell them of Jesus, the mighty to save.

Down in the human heart, crushed by the tempter, feelings lie
buried that grace can restore; touched by a loving heart, wakened
by kindness, chords that are broken will vibrate once more.

Rescue the perishing, duty demands it; strength for thy
labor the Lord will provide; back to the narrow way patiently
win them; tell the poor wand'rer a Savior has died.

Rescue the perishing, care for the dying; Jesus
is merciful, Jesus will save.

Reflect seriously that it is the divine image in every person (Genesis 1:26, 27) that gives life an intrinsic dignity and worth

—regardless of race, color, sex, age, or social standing. That's what makes each person worthy of being rescued from eternal damnation. Sing this musical challenge as you go—

ΔΔΔ

LUKE 14

"Don't begin until you count the cost"

LUKE 14 (NLT)

New Living Translation

One Sabbath day Jesus went to eat dinner in the home of a leader of the Pharisees, and the people were watching him closely. There was a man there whose arms and legs were swollen. Jesus asked the Pharisees and experts in religious law, "Is it permitted in the law to heal people on the Sabbath day, or not?" When they refused to answer, Jesus touched the sick man and healed him and sent him away.

Then he turned to them and said, "Which of you doesn't work on the Sabbath? If your son or your cow falls into a pit, don't you rush to get him out?" Again they could not answer.

When Jesus noticed that all who had come to the dinner were trying to sit in the seats of honor near the head of the table, he gave them this advice: "When you are invited to a wedding feast, don't sit in the seat of honor. What if someone who is more distinguished than you has also been invited? The host will come and say, 'Give this person your seat.' Then you will be embarrassed, and you will have to take whatever seat is left at the foot of the table! Instead, take the lowest place at the foot of the table. Then when your host sees you, he will come and say, 'Friend, we have a better place for you!' Then you will be honored in front of all the other guests. For those who exalt themselves will be humbled, and those who humble themselves will be exalted." Then he turned to his host. "When you put on a luncheon or a banquet," he said, "don't invite your friends, brothers, relatives, and rich neighbors. For they will invite you back, and that will be your only reward. Instead, invite the poor, the crippled, the lame, and the blind. Then at the resurrection of the righteous, God will reward you for inviting those who could not repay you."

Hearing this, a man sitting at the table with Jesus exclaimed, "What a blessing it will be to attend a banquet in the Kingdom of God!"

Jesus replied with this story: "A man prepared a great feast and sent out many invitations. When the banquet was ready, he sent his servant to tell the guests, 'Come, the banquet is ready.' But they all began making excuses. One said, 'I have just bought a field and must inspect it. Please excuse me.' Another said, 'I have just bought five pairs of oxen, and I want to try them out. Please excuse me.' Another said, 'I just got married, so I can't come.' The servant returned and told his master what they had said. His master was furious and said, 'Go quickly into the streets and alleys of the town and invite the poor, the crippled, the blind, and the lame.' After the servant had done this, he reported, 'There is still room for more.' So his master said, 'Go out into the country lanes and behind the hedges and urge anyone you find to come, so that the house will be full. For none of those I first invited will get even the smallest taste of my banquet.' "

A large crowd was following Jesus. He turned around and said to them, "If you want to be my disciple, you must, by comparison, hate everyone else—your father and mother, wife and children, brothers and sisters—yes, even your own life. Otherwise, you cannot be my disciple. And if you do not carry your own cross and follow me, you cannot be my disciple. But don't begin until you count the cost. For who would begin construction of a building without first calculating the cost to see if there is enough money to finish it? Otherwise, you might complete only the foundation before running out of money, and then everyone would laugh at you. They would say, 'There's the person who started that building and couldn't afford to finish it!'

"Or what king would go to war against another king without first sitting down with his counselors to discuss whether his army of 10,000 could defeat the 20,000 soldiers marching against him? And if he can't, he will send a delegation to discuss terms of peace while the enemy is still far away. So you cannot become my disciple without giving up everything you own. Salt is good for seasoning. But if it loses its flavor, how do you make it salty again? Flavorless salt is good neither for the soil nor for the manure pile. It is thrown away. Anyone with ears to hear should listen and understand!"

ΔΔΔ

MANUSCRIPT

BIBLE STUDY METHOD

The Manuscript Bible study method eliminates verse numbers and paragraph headings so we can focus on just the scripture itself.

In Luke 7, we learned about the Manuscript Bible study method. So, you probably were not surprise to discover that Luke 14 didn't include any paragraph headings or verse numbers—as this is the distinguishing characteristic of a Manuscript Bible Study.

In a Manuscript study, you start with the basic text of the Bible with nothing else added—since chapter numbers, verse numbers, punctuation, and paragraph headings were actually added years later to our translations. What next?

Look For The W's:

Who is involved? *When* did it happen? *Where* is it happening? *What* is taking place? Ask yourself a few *why* questions regarding what Luke 14 is about.

Mark It Up!

Use a variety of colored pens and pencils to mark up Luke 14. (You may want to employ a bit of the C.U.B.E method we looked at with Luke 6 and Luke 13, and perhaps throw in a few other shapes—such as squiggly lines or smily faces—that make sense to you). Don't worry about getting it "right," just mark it up.

Reflect, Pray, Act.

How does what you're reading and studying apply to you and where you are with God, others, etc.?

CARRY THE CROSS

DEVOTIONAL READING

May 13, June 20, and December 23 readings of Samuel G. Hardman and Dwight Lyman Moody, Thoughts for the Quiet Hour (Willow Grove, PA: Woodlawn Electronic Publishing, 1997).

"...take the lowest place at the foot of the table..." (Luke 14:10, NLT)

"**H**e who is willing to take the lowest place will always find sitting room; there is no great crush for the worst places. There is nothing like the jostling at the back that there is at the front; so if we would be comfortable, we shall do well to keep behind." — Thomas Champness

"For those who exalt themselves will be humbled, and those who humble themselves will be exalted." (Luke 14:11, NLT)

"... If you ask the way to the crown 'tis by the cross; to the mountain—'tis by the valley; to exaltation—'tis he that humbleth himself." — J. H. Evans

"And if you do not carry your own cross and follow me, you cannot be my disciple." (Luke 14:27, NLT)

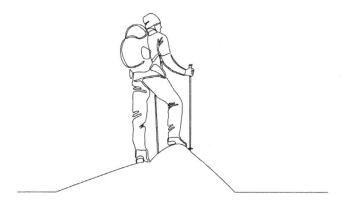

"There is always the shadow of the cross resting upon the Christian's path. Is that a reason why you should avoid or not undertake the duty? Have you made up your mind that you will follow your Master everywhere else, save when He ascends the path that leads to the cross? Is that your religion? The sooner you change it, the better. The religion of the Lord Jesus Christ is the religion of the cross, and unless we take up our cross, we can never follow Him." — W. Hay Aitken

ΔΔΔ

LUKE 15

"Everything I have is yours"

LUKE 15 (NIRV)

New International Reader's Version

THE STORY OF THE LOST SHEEP

The tax collectors and "sinners" were all gathering around to hear Jesus.

2 But the Pharisees and the teachers of the law were whispering among themselves. They said, "This man welcomes sinners and eats with them."

3 Then Jesus told them a story.

4 He said, "Suppose one of you has 100 sheep and loses one of them. Won't he leave the 99 in the open country? Won't he go and look for the one lost sheep until he finds it?

5 When he finds it, he will joyfully put it on his shoulders

6 and go home. Then he will call his friends and neighbors together. He will say, 'Be joyful with me. I have found my lost sheep.'

7 "I tell you, it will be the same in heaven. There will be great joy when one sinner turns away from sin. Yes, there will be more joy than for 99 godly people who do not need to turn away from their sins.

THE STORY OF THE LOST COIN

8 "Or suppose a woman has ten silver coins and loses one. She will light a lamp and sweep the house. She will search carefully until she finds the coin.

9 And when she finds it, she will call her friends and neighbors together. She will say, 'Be joyful with me. I have found my lost coin.'

10 "I tell you, it is the same in heaven. There is joy in heaven over one sinner who turns away from sin."

THE STORY OF THE LOST SON

11 Jesus continued, "There was a man who had two sons.

12 The younger son spoke to his father. He said, 'Father, give me my share of the family property.' So the father divided his property between his two sons.

13 "Not long after that, the younger son packed up all he had. Then he left for a country far away. There he wasted his money on wild living.

14 He spent everything he had. "Then the whole country ran low on food. So the son didn't have what he needed.

15 He went to work for someone who lived in that country, who sent him to the fields to feed the pigs.

16 The son wanted to fill his stomach with the food the pigs were eating. But no one gave him anything.

17 "Then he began to think clearly again. He said, 'How many of my father's hired workers have more than enough food! But here I am dying from hunger!

18 I will get up and go back to my father. I will say to him, "Father, I have sinned against heaven. And I have sinned against you.

19 I am no longer fit to be called your son. Make me like one of your hired workers."'

20 So he got up and went to his father. "While the son was still a long way off, his father saw him. He was filled with tender love for his son. He ran to him. He threw his arms around him and kissed him.

21 "The son said to him, 'Father, I have sinned against heaven and against you. I am no longer fit to be called your son.'

22 "But the father said to his servants, 'Quick! Bring the best robe and put it on him. Put a ring on his finger and sandals on his feet.

23 Bring the fattest calf and kill it. Let's have a big dinner and celebrate.

24 This son of mine was dead. And now he is alive again. He was lost. And now he is found.' "So they began to celebrate.

25 "The older son was in the field. When he came near the house, he heard music and dancing.

26 So he called one of the servants. He asked him what was going on.

27 " 'Your brother has come home,' the servant replied. 'Your father has killed the fattest calf. He has done this because your brother is back safe and sound.'

28 "The older brother became angry. He refused to go in. So his father went out and begged him.

29 "But he answered his father, 'Look! All these years I've worked like a slave for you. I have always obeyed your orders. You never gave me even a young goat so I could celebrate with my friends.

30 But this son of yours wasted your money with some prostitutes. Now he comes home. And for him you kill the fattest calf!'

31 " 'My son,' the father said, 'you are always with me. Everything I have is yours.

32 But we had to celebrate and be glad. This brother of yours was dead. And now he is alive again. He was lost. And now he is found.' "

∆∆∆

S.O.A.P.

BIBLE STUDY METHOD

You're practically an expert with S.O.A.P. now, since this is the method we employed in Luke 1 and Luke 8. So, let's get right to it.

1. Study

Study the scripture. You've already done this, but consider taking the time to reread Luke 15. Ask the Holy Spirit to illuminate what He would like you to see. Highlight words or phrases that stand out to you.

2. Observe

Make some observations. Is there anything in Luke 15 you've never noticed before? What is the context of this passage? (In other words, what comes before and after these verses)? Are there any specific words or phrases that stand out to you? Does this passage remind you of any other Bible passages?

3. Apply

For this step, ask yourself one simple question, "What is the Holy Spirit saying to me through the verses of Luke 15?" Take a moment to quiet yourself, and listen for God's voice. He may have something to say regarding your thoughts, your actions, your relationships, your plans, your dreams—and unless we consciously take the time to *just listen*, we may miss out on what he has to say.

4. Pray

Your prayer could include things like: thanking God for the truths that He highlighted during your study of Luke 15, thanking him for what he helped you to observe, and asking for his help to apply these truths and observations to your life.

THIS MAN RECEIVETH SINNERS

DEVOTIONAL READING

September 13 reading of C. H. Spurgeon, Morning and Evening: Daily Readings (London: Passmore & Alabaster, 1896).

"But the Pharisees and the teachers of the law were whispering among themselves. They said, "This man welcomes sinners and eats with them." (Luke 15:2, NiRV)

Observe the condescension of this fact. This Man, who towers above all other men, holy, harmless, undefiled, and separate from sinners—this Man receiveth sinners. This Man, who is no other than the eternal God, before whom angels veil their faces—this Man receiveth sinners. It needs an angel's tongue to describe such a mighty stoop of love.

That any of *us* should be willing to seek after the lost is nothing wonderful—they are of our own race; but that he, the offended God, against whom the transgression has been committed, should take upon himself the form of a servant, and bear the sin of many, and should then be willing to receive the vilest of the vile, this is marvelous.

"This Man receiveth sinners"; not, however, that they may remain sinners, but he receives them that he may pardon their sins, justify their persons, cleanse their hearts by his purifying word, preserve their souls by the indwelling of the Holy Ghost, and enable them to serve him, to show forth his praise, and to have communion with him.

Into his heart's love he receives sinners, takes them from the dunghill, and wears them as jewels in his crown; plucks them as brands from the burning, and preserves them as costly monuments of his mercy. None are so precious in Jesus' sight as the sinners for whom he died.

When Jesus receives sinners, he has not some out-of-doors reception place, no casual ward where he charitably entertains them as men do passing beggars, but he opens the golden gates of his royal heart, and receives the sinner right into himself —yea, he admits the humble penitent into personal union and makes him a member of his body, of his flesh, and of his bones. There was never such a reception as this!

This fact is still most sure, he is still receiving sinners: would to God sinners would receive him.

LUKE 16

"No worker can serve two bosses"

LUKE 16 (MSG)

The Message

THE STORY OF THE CROOKED MANAGER

Jesus said to his disciples, "There was once a rich man who had a manager. He got reports that the manager had been taking advantage of his position by running up huge personal expenses. So he called him in and said, 'What's this I hear about you? You're fired. And I want a complete audit of your books.'

3-4 "The manager said to himself, 'What am I going to do? I've lost my job as manager. I'm not strong enough for a laboring job, and I'm too proud to beg.... Ah, I've got a plan. Here's what I'll do ... then when I'm turned out into the street, people will take me into their houses.'

5 "Then he went at it. One after another, he called in the people who were in debt to his master. He said to the first, 'How much do you owe my master?'

6 "He replied, 'A hundred jugs of olive oil.'

"The manager said, 'Here, take your bill, sit down here—quick now—write fifty.'

7 "To the next he said, 'And you, what do you owe?'

"He answered, 'A hundred sacks of wheat.'

"He said, 'Take your bill, write in eighty.'

8-9 "Now here's a surprise: The master praised the crooked manager! And why? Because he knew how to look after himself. Streetwise people are smarter in this regard than law-abiding citizens. They are on constant alert, looking for angles, surviving by their wits. I want you to be smart in the same way —but for what is right—using every adversity to stimulate you to creative survival, to concentrate your attention on the bare essentials, so you'll live, really live, and not complacently just get by on good behavior."

GOD SEES BEHIND APPEARANCES

10-13 Jesus went on to make these comments:
If you're honest in small things,
you'll be honest in big things;
If you're a crook in small things,
you'll be a crook in big things.
If you're not honest in small jobs,
who will put you in charge of the store?
No worker can serve two bosses:
He'll either hate the first and love the second
Or adore the first and despise the second.
You can't serve both God and the Bank.

14-18 When the Pharisees, a money-obsessed bunch, heard him say these things, they rolled their eyes, dismissing him as hopelessly out of touch. So Jesus spoke to them: "You are masters at making yourselves look good in front of others, but God knows what's behind the appearance.
What society sees and calls monumental,

God sees through and calls monstrous.
God's Law and the Prophets climaxed in John;
Now it's all kingdom of God—the glad news
and compelling invitation to every man and woman.
The sky will disintegrate and the earth dissolve
before a single letter of God's Law wears out.
Using the legalities of divorce
as a cover for lust is adultery;
Using the legalities of marriage
as a cover for lust is adultery.

THE RICH MAN AND LAZARUS

19-21 "There once was a rich man, expensively dressed in the latest fashions, wasting his days in conspicuous consumption. A poor man named Lazarus, covered with sores, had been dumped on his doorstep. All he lived for was to get a meal from scraps off the rich man's table. His best friends were the dogs who came and licked his sores.

22-24 "Then he died, this poor man, and was taken up by the angels to the lap of Abraham. The rich man also died and was buried. In hell and in torment, he looked up and saw Abraham in the distance and Lazarus in his lap. He called out, 'Father Abraham, mercy! Have mercy! Send Lazarus to dip his finger in water to cool my tongue. I'm in agony in this fire.'

25-26 "But Abraham said, 'Child, remember that in your lifetime you got the good things and Lazarus the bad things. It's not like that here. Here he's consoled and you're tormented. Besides, in all these matters there is a huge chasm set between us so that no one can go from us to you even if he wanted to, nor can anyone cross over from you to us.'

27-28 "The rich man said, 'Then let me ask you, Father: Send him to the house of my father where I have five brothers, so he can tell them the score and warn them so they won't end up here in this place of torment.'

29 "Abraham answered, 'They have Moses and the Prophets to tell them the score. Let them listen to them.'

30 " 'I know, Father Abraham,' he said, 'but they're not listening. If someone came back to them from the dead, they would change their ways.'

31 "Abraham replied, 'If they won't listen to Moses and the Prophets, they're not going to be convinced by someone who rises from the dead.' "

ΔΔΔ

R.E.A.P.

BIBLE STUDY METHOD

*We've already employed R.E.A.P. method in Luke 2
and Luke 9, so let's get right to it.*

1. Read

Take a few moments to *reread* the Luke 16. Ask the Holy Spirit
to illuminate what He would like you to see. Highlight words or
phrases that stand out to you.

2. Examine

Ask yourself a few questions, such as: What is going on in Luke
16? What are the circumstances? Who are the main characters?
What are the major themes? What is the context? Are there any
specific words or phrases that stand out to me? Does Luke 16

remind me of any other Bible passages?

3. Apply

Here's a few simple questions you can ask to help you apply this (and any) passage: Is there a truth to believe? A sin to repent of? A promise to claim? A command to follow? What are things that need to change in light of this text? How will I live differently and be different because of what I just read? What is the Holy Spirit saying to me through these verses?

4. Pray

Your prayer could include things like: thanking God for the truths that He highlighted in your reading, thanking him for what he helped you to examine, and asking for his help to apply these to your life.

INTEGRITY WITH MONEY

DEVOTIONAL READING

From the April 14 reading of bibleinoneyear.org by Nicky Gumbel

Jesus spoke about money more than virtually any other subject (including prayer and heaven). Twelve out of his thirty-eight parables are about money or possessions. As Billy Graham put it, 'If a person gets their attitude towards money straight, it will help straighten out almost every other area in their life.'

In today's passage, Jesus teaches us how to get a right view of money. He starts with the rather strange parable of the dishonest manager, who is commended for his shrewdness.

1. Money Is A Tool

The people of this world are often more sensible, thoughtful, prudent and wise than the people of God in understanding that money is *a tool.* The dishonest manager is commended for his shrewdness in seeing this. The reality is that money can be a tool for eternal benefit. *'I tell you, use worldly wealth to gain friends for yourselves, so that when it is gone, you will be welcomed into eternal dwellings'* (v.9, NIV).

Jesus taught on the wonder of being with him for eternity in the parables of the great banquet (14:15–24) and the prodigal son (15:11–32). Here, we are reminded that the use of our money on earth can have eternal consequences. One of Jesus' primary concerns was to see the good news of the kingdom of God being preached (16:16). Your money can be used to see God's rule and reign coming in to people's lives – with eternal consequences.

2. Money Is A Test

Jesus is not commending the dishonest manager for his dishonesty. Indeed, the opposite is the case. He goes on to say, 'If you're honest in small things, you'll be honest in big things; If you're a crook in small things, you'll be a crook in big things. If you're not honest in small jobs, who will put you in charge of the store?' (vv.10–11, MSG).

Be an honest and trustworthy steward of everything God has given you, including your money. The more trustworthy you are with money, the more God will give you 'true riches'.

3. Money Is A Threat

Jesus says, '*No worker can serve two bosses: he'll either hate the first and love the second or adore the first and despise the second. You can't serve both God and the Bank.*' (v.13). As Dietrich Bonhoeffer put it, 'Our hearts have room for only one all-embracing devotion, and we can only cleave to one Lord.'

Money is to be used, but not loved. Don't love money and use people. Love people and use money.

The threat is that love of money leads to hatred of God (v.13). The Pharisees loved money (they were 'money-obsessed', MSG) and sneered at Jesus (v.14). Have the opposite attitude to money. 'Despise' it (v.13). In other words, treat it with contempt by giving generously and focusing your love not on money, but on

God who 'knows your hearts' (v.15).

> Lord, help me to be a good steward of everything that you have entrusted to me, to be honest and trustworthy. Help me to give generously and focus my thoughts not on money but on you.

LUKE 17

"Increase our faith!"

LUKE 17 (NIV)

New International Version

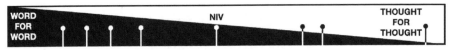

SIN, FAITH, AND DUTY

Jesus said to his disciples: "Things that cause people to stumble are bound to come, but woe to anyone through whom they come.

2 It would be better for them to be thrown into the sea with a millstone tied around their neck than to cause one of these little ones to stumble.

3 So watch yourselves. "If your brother or sister sins against you, rebuke them; and if they repent, forgive them.

4 Even if they sin against you seven times in a day and seven times come back to you saying 'I repent,' you must forgive them."

5 The apostles said to the Lord, "Increase our faith!"

6 He replied, "If you have faith as small as a mustard seed, you can say to this mulberry tree, 'Be uprooted and planted in the sea,' and it will obey you.

7 "Suppose one of you has a servant plowing or looking after the sheep. Will he say to the servant when he comes in from the field, 'Come along now and sit down to eat'?

8 Won't he rather say, 'Prepare my supper, get yourself ready and wait on me while I eat and drink; after that you may eat and drink'?

9 Will he thank the servant because he did what he was told to do?

10 So you also, when you have done everything you were told to do, should say, 'We are unworthy servants; we have only done our duty.' "

JESUS HEALS TEN MEN WITH LEPROSY

11 Now on his way to Jerusalem, Jesus traveled along the border between Samaria and Galilee.

12 As he was going into a village, ten men who had leprosy met him. They stood at a distance

13 and called out in a loud voice, "Jesus, Master, have pity on us!"

14 When he saw them, he said, "Go, show yourselves to the priests." And as they went, they were cleansed.

15 One of them, when he saw he was healed, came back, praising God in a loud voice.

16 He threw himself at Jesus' feet and thanked him—and he was a Samaritan.

THE COMING OF THE KINGDOM OF GOD

17 Jesus asked, "Were not all ten cleansed? Where are the other nine?

18 Has no one returned to give praise to God except this foreigner?"

19 Then he said to him, "Rise and go; your faith has made you well."

20 Once, on being asked by the Pharisees when the kingdom of God would come, Jesus replied, "The coming of the kingdom of

God is not something that can be observed,

21 nor will people say, 'Here it is,' or 'There it is,' because the kingdom of God is in your midst."

22 Then he said to his disciples, "The time is coming when you will long to see one of the days of the Son of Man, but you will not see it.

23 People will tell you, 'There he is!' or 'Here he is!' Do not go running off after them.

24 For the Son of Man in his day will be like the lightning, which flashes and lights up the sky from one end to the other.

25 But first he must suffer many things and be rejected by this generation.

26 "Just as it was in the days of Noah, so also will it be in the days of the Son of Man.

27 People were eating, drinking, marrying and being given in marriage up to the day Noah entered the ark. Then the flood came and destroyed them all.

28 "It was the same in the days of Lot. People were eating and drinking, buying and selling, planting and building.

29 But the day Lot left Sodom, fire and sulfur rained down from heaven and destroyed them all.

30 "It will be just like this on the day the Son of Man is revealed.

31 On that day no one who is on the housetop, with possessions inside, should go down to get them. Likewise, no one in the field should go back for anything.

32 Remember Lot's wife!

33 Whoever tries to keep their life will lose it, and whoever loses their life will preserve it.

34 I tell you, on that night two people will be in one bed; one will be taken and the other left.

35 Two women will be grinding grain together; one will be taken and the other left."

37 "Where, Lord?" they asked. He replied, "Where there is a dead body, there the vultures will gather."

ΔΔΔ

4R'S

BIBLE STUDY METHOD

Surely by now, you've noticed a patter when it comes to Bible study. We may use different terminology (such as S.O.A.P or R.E.A.P., etc.), but the basics remain the same: we read, reflect, respond and rest in His Word.

1. Read

Time to *reread* Luke 17. Ask the Holy Spirit to illuminate what He would like you to see. Highlight words or phrases that stand out to you.

2. Reflect

What is Luke 17 saying to you? What did you hear, or what are you feeling or thinking? What is the context? Are there any specific words or phrases that stand out to me? Does tLuke 17 remind me of any other Bible passages?

3. Respond

What is your response to Luke 17? Ask yourself one simple question, "What is the Holy Spirit saying to me through these verses?" Take a moment to quiet yourself, and listen for God's voice. He may have something to say regarding your thoughts, your actions, your relationships, your plans, and your dreams.

4. Rest

Quietly ponder what you've read, and how you've chosen to respond—trusting God for the strength and courage necessary.

O FOR A FAITH THAT WILL NOT SHRINK

DEVOTIONAL READING

October 26 reading of Kenneth W. Osbeck, Amazing Grace: 366 Inspiring Hymn Stories for Daily Devotions (Grand Rapids, MI: Kregel Publications, 1996), 321.

"The apostles said to the Lord, "Increase our faith!" He replied, "If you have faith as small as a mustard seed, you can say to this mulberry tree, 'Be uprooted and planted in the sea,' and it will obey you." (Luke 17:5–6, NIV)

"When the world seems at its worst, Christians must be at their best."—Unknown

"Faith is to believe what we do not see, and the reward of faith is to see what we believe."—St. Augustine

Discouragement can easily cause our faith to shrink, and we may even at times consider quitting our service for God. Perhaps we have all experienced these sentiments:

"I've taught a class for many years; borne many burdens, toiled through tears—But folks don't notice me a bit, I'm so discouraged, I'll just quit."—Unknown

One of the chief characteristics of spiritual maturity is the ability to persevere—even in the face of adversity. God often permits difficulties to come into our lives simply to allow our faith in Him to become stronger. A faith that is never tested and strengthened soon becomes a shrinking one. But if our faith is real, it will stand every test and prove to be an overcoming faith.

This hymn text, which is an exposition of Luke 17:5, is from William Bathurst's Psalms and Hymns for Public and Private Use. The song was originally titled "The Power of Faith." The first three stanzas describe a victorious faith amidst some of the most difficult circumstances in life. The final stanza affirms the believer's desire to have such trust that even now life becomes a foretaste of heaven itself.

William Hiley Bathurst was an Anglican minister who wrote more than 200 hymn texts. The composer of the music, William H. Havergal, the father of Frances Ridley Havergal, was also prominent in the Church of England, as a minister and writer of many hymns.

> O for a faith that will not shrink tho pressed by many a foe,
> that will not tremble on the brink of any earthly woe.
>
> That will not murmur nor complain beneath the chast'ning
> rod, but in the hour of grief or pain will lean upon its God.
>
> A faith that shines more bright and clear when tempests rage without,
> that, when in danger, knows no fear, in darkness feels no doubt.
>
> Lord, give me such a faith as this, and then, whate'er may come,
> I'll taste e'en now the hallowed bliss of an eternal home.

Ponder this question—Could I stand to lose everything and still have an implicit faith in God and know with certainty that He is in absolute control?

Carry this musical resolve—"O For a Faith That Will Not

Shrink."

LUKE 18

"Things which are impossible with men are possible with God"

LUKE 18 (KJV)

King James Version

THE PARABLE OF THE WOMAN AND THE JUDGE

And he spake a parable unto them to this end, that men ought always to pray, and not to faint;

2 Saying, There was in a city a judge, which feared not God, neither regarded man:

3 And there was a widow in that city; and she came unto him, saying, Avenge me of mine adversary.

4 And he would not for a while: but afterward he said within himself, Though I fear not God, nor regard man;

5 Yet because this widow troubleth me, I will avenge her, lest by her continual coming she weary me.

6 And the Lord said, Hear what the unjust judge saith.

7 And shall not God avenge his own elect, which cry day and night unto him, though he bear long with them?

8 I tell you that he will avenge them speedily. Nevertheless when the Son of man cometh, shall he find faith on the earth?

THE PARABLE OF THE PHARISEE AND THE TAX COLLECTOR

9 And he spake this parable unto certain which trusted in themselves that they were righteous, and despised others:

10 Two men went up into the temple to pray; the one a Pharisee,

and the other a publican.

11 The Pharisee stood and prayed thus with himself, God, I thank thee, that I am not as other men are, extortioners, unjust, adulterers, or even as this publican.

12 I fast twice in the week, I give tithes of all that I possess.

13 And the publican, standing afar off, would not lift up so much as his eyes unto heaven, but smote upon his breast, saying, God be merciful to me a sinner.

14 I tell you, this man went down to his house justified rather than the other: for every one that exalteth himself shall be abased; and he that humbleth himself shall be exalted.

CHRIST BLESSED THE CHILDREN

15 And they brought unto him also infants, that he would touch them: but when his disciples saw it, they rebuked them.

16 But Jesus called them unto him, and said, Suffer little children to come unto me, and forbid them not: for of such is the kingdom of God.

17 Verily I say unto you, Whosoever shall not receive the kingdom of God as a little child shall in no wise enter therein.

RICH YOUNG RULER

18 And a certain ruler asked him, saying, Good Master, what shall I do to inherit eternal life?

19 And Jesus said unto him, Why callest thou me good? none is good, save one, that is, God.

20 Thou knowest the commandments, Do not commit adultery, Do not kill, Do not steal, Do not bear false witness, Honour thy father and thy mother.

21 And he said, All these have I kept from my youth up.

22 Now when Jesus heard these things, he said unto him, Yet lackest thou one thing: sell all that thou hast, and distribute unto the poor, and thou shalt have treasure in heaven: and come, follow me.

23 And when he heard this, he was very sorrowful: for he was very rich.

24 And when Jesus saw that he was very sorrowful, he said, How hardly shall they that have riches enter into the kingdom of God!

25 For it is easier for a camel to go through a needle's eye, than for a rich man to enter into the kingdom of God.

26 And they that heard it said, Who then can be saved?

27 And he said, The things which are impossible with men are possible with God.

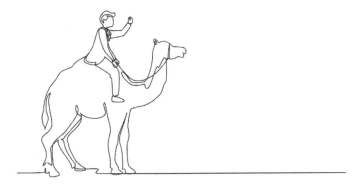

CHRIST WILL REWARD SACRIFICE

28 Then Peter said, Lo, we have left all, and followed thee.

29 And he said unto them, Verily I say unto you, There is no man that hath left house, or parents, or brethren, or wife, or children, for the kingdom of God's sake,

30 Who shall not receive manifold more in this present time, and in the world to come life everlasting.

CHRIST FORETELLS HIS DEATH AND RESURRECTION

31 Then he took unto him the twelve, and said unto them, Behold, we go up to Jerusalem, and all things that are written by the prophets concerning the Son of man shall be accomplished.

32 For he shall be delivered unto the Gentiles, and shall be mocked, and spitefully entreated, and spitted on:

33 And they shall scourge him, and put him to death: and the third day he shall rise again.

34 And they understood none of these things: and this saying was hid from them, neither knew they the things which were spoken.

CHRIST HEALS BARTIMAEUS

35 And it came to pass, that as he was come nigh unto Jericho, a certain blind man sat by the way side begging:

36 And hearing the multitude pass by, he asked what it meant.

37 And they told him, that Jesus of Nazareth passeth by.

38 And he cried, saying, Jesus, thou Son of David, have mercy on me.

39 And they which went before rebuked him, that he should hold his peace: but he cried so much the more, Thou Son of David, have mercy on me.

40 And Jesus stood, and commanded him to be brought unto him: and when he was come near, he asked him,

41 Saying, What wilt thou that I shall do unto thee? And he said, Lord, that I may receive my sight.

42 And Jesus said unto him, Receive thy sight: thy faith hath saved thee.

43 And immediately he received his sight, and followed him, glorifying God: and all the people, when they saw it, gave praise unto God.

∆∆∆

C.O.R.E.

BIBLE STUDY METHOD

We're back to my personal favorite: C.O.R.E. We used this method in both Luke 4 and Luke 11. If you enjoy creating content, this method can provide a great structure for a devotional, blog post, or short video.

1. Catalytic Question

Consider taking a moment to reread Luke 18. As you do, see if there is a big question that Luke 18 seems to be answering. This big question is your *Catalytic* Question—the kind of question that sparks additional thoughts.

2. Objective Sentence

The objective sentence is your *answer* to the catalytic question, which is based on what you just read in Luke 18. (See Luke 4 and 11 for examples).

3. Rationale

The Rationale is where you provide more details to the objective sentence. (See Luke 4 and 11 for examples).

4. Express Thanks

Take a moment to express thanks to God for what he has shown you in his Word today.

PERSEVERANCE IN PRAYER

DEVOTIONAL READING

November 17 Reading of Lettie B. Cowman, Streams in the Desert (Los Angeles, CA: The Oriental Missionary Society, 1925), 113–114.

"And the Lord said, Hear what the unjust judge saith. And shall not God avenge his own elect, which cry day and night unto him, though he bear long with them?" (Luke 18:6–7, AV)

GOD'S seasons are not at your beck. If the first stroke doth not bring forth the fire, you must strike again. God will hear prayer, but He may not answer it at the time which we in our minds have appointed; He will reveal Himself to our seeking hearts, but not just when and where we have settled in our own expectations. Hence the need of perseverance and importunity in supplication.

In the days of flint and steel and brimstone matches we had to strike and strike again, dozens of times, before we could get a spark to live in the tinder; and we were thankful enough if we succeeded at last.

Shall we not be as persevering and hopeful as to heavenly things? We have more certainty of success in this business than we had with our flint and steel, for we have God's promises at our back.

> Never let us despair. God's time for mercy will come; yea, it has come, if our time for believing has arrived. Ask in faith, nothing wavering; but never cease from petitioning because the King delays to reply. Strike the steel again. Make the sparks fly and have your tinder ready; you will get a light before long.—C. H. Spurgeon.

> I do not believe that there is such a thing in the history of God's kingdom as a right prayer offered in a right spirit that is forever left unanswered.—Theodore L. Cuyler.

LUKE 19

"The Son of Man has come to seek and to save"

LUKE 19 (NKJV)

New King James Version

CHRIST ABIDES WITH ZACCHAEUS

Then Jesus entered and passed through Jericho.

2 Now behold, there was a man named Zacchaeus who was a chief tax collector, and he was rich.

3 And he sought to see who Jesus was, but could not because of the crowd, for he was of short stature.

4 So he ran ahead and climbed up into a sycamore tree to see Him, for He was going to pass that way.

5 And when Jesus came to the place, He looked up and saw him, and said to him, "Zacchaeus, make haste and come down, for today I must stay at your house."

6 So he made haste and came down, and received Him joyfully.

7 But when they saw it, they all complained, saying, "He has gone to be a guest with a man who is a sinner."

8 Then Zacchaeus stood and said to the Lord, "Look, Lord, I give half of my goods to the poor; and if I have taken anything from anyone by false accusation, I restore fourfold."

9 And Jesus said to him, "Today salvation has come to this house, because he also is a son of Abraham;

10 for the Son of Man has come to seek and to save that which was lost."

CHRIST GIVES THE PARABLE OF THE TEN MINAS

11 Now as they heard these things, He spoke another parable, because He was near Jerusalem and because they thought the kingdom of God would appear immediately.

12 Therefore He said: "A certain nobleman went into a far country to receive for himself a kingdom and to return.

13 So he called ten of his servants, delivered to them ten minas, and said to them, 'Do business till I come.'

14 But his citizens hated him, and sent a delegation after him, saying, 'We will not have this man to reign over us.'

15 "And so it was that when he returned, having received the kingdom, he then commanded these servants, to whom he had given the money, to be called to him, that he might know how much every man had gained by trading.

16 Then came the first, saying, 'Master, your mina has earned ten minas.'

17 And he said to him, 'Well done, good servant; because you were faithful in a very little, have authority over ten cities.'

18 And the second came, saying, 'Master, your mina has earned five minas.'

19 Likewise he said to him, 'You also be over five cities.'

20 "Then another came, saying, 'Master, here is your mina, which I have kept put away in a handkerchief.

21 For I feared you, because you are an austere man. You collect what you did not deposit, and reap what you did not sow.'

22 And he said to him, 'Out of your own mouth I will judge you, you wicked servant. You knew that I was an austere man, collecting what I did not deposit and reaping what I did not sow.

23 Why then did you not put my money in the bank, that at my coming I might have collected it with interest?'

24 "And he said to those who stood by, 'Take the mina from him, and give it to him who has ten minas.'

25 (But they said to him, 'Master, he has ten minas.')

26 'For I say to you, that to everyone who has will be given; and from him who does not have, even what he has will be taken away from him.

27 But bring here those enemies of mine, who did not want me to reign over them, and slay them before me.' "

THE TRIUMPHAL ENTRY

28 When He had said this, He went on ahead, going up to Jerusalem.

29 And it came to pass, when He drew near to Bethphage and Bethany, at the mountain called Olivet, that He sent two of His disciples,

30 saying, "Go into the village opposite you, where as you enter you will find a colt tied, on which no one has ever sat. Loose it and bring it here.

31 And if anyone asks you, 'Why are you loosing it?' thus you shall say to him, 'Because the Lord has need of it.' "

32 So those who were sent went their way and found it just as He had said to them.

33 But as they were loosing the colt, the owners of it said to them, "Why are you loosing the colt?"

34 And they said, "The Lord has need of him."

35 Then they brought him to Jesus. And they threw their own clothes on the colt, and they set Jesus on him.

36 And as He went, many spread their clothes on the road.

37 Then, as He was now drawing near the descent of the Mount of Olives, the whole multitude of the disciples began to rejoice and praise God with a loud voice for all the mighty works they had seen,

38 saying: " 'Blessed is the King who comes in the name of the Lord!' Peace in heaven and glory in the highest!"

39 And some of the Pharisees called to Him from the crowd, "Teacher, rebuke Your disciples."

40 But He answered and said to them, "I tell you that if these should keep silent, the stones would immediately cry out."

41 Now as He drew near, He saw the city and wept over it,

42 saying, "If you had known, even you, especially in this your day, the things that make for your peace! But now they are hidden from your eyes.

43 For days will come upon you when your enemies will build an embankment around you, surround you and close you in on every side,

44 and level you, and your children within you, to the ground; and they will not leave in you one stone upon another, because you did not know the time of your visitation."

CLEANSING THE TEMPLE

45 Then He went into the temple and began to drive out those who bought and sold in it,

46 saying to them, "It is written, 'My house is a house of prayer,' but you have made it a 'den of thieves.' "

47 And He was teaching daily in the temple. But the chief priests, the scribes, and the leaders of the people sought to destroy Him,

48 and were unable to do anything; for all the people were very attentive to hear Him.

ΔΔΔ

DISCOVERY

BIBLE STUDY METHOD

We discovered the Discovery Bible Study (DBS) method back in Luke 5 and Luke 12. DBS is question-based Bible study that encourages the Bible discovery, obedience to what is learned, and sharing it with others.

Read

After reading Luke 19, answer the following questions.

Questions

1. What does Luke 19 tell me about God and/or His plan?

2. What does Luke 19 tell me about people?

3. If Luke 19 is truly from God, how will I apply and obey it? (Begin your answer by saying, "I will...")

4. Who needs to hear Luke 19, and when will I share it?

PASS IT ON

DEVOTIONAL READING

Day 108 reading of John Baker and Johnny Baker, Celebrate Recovery Daily Devotional: 366 Devotionals (Grand Rapids, MI: Zondervan, 2013).

"And Jesus said to him, "Today salvation has come to this house, because he also is a son of Abraham; for the Son of Man has come to seek and to save that which was lost."" (Luke 19:9–10, NKJV)

I was in the drive-thru line at Starbucks thinking about the great cup of coffee I had just ordered—a triple shot of espresso, caramel macchiato, venti, skinny, at 180 degrees. Actually, I was thinking that just learning how to place my Starbucks order was quite an accomplishment!

As I pulled up to the window, money in hand, the friendly cashier said, "The car in front of you paid for yours." I was taken aback by this unsolicited act of kindness and wrestled with what to do. Just thanking the cashier didn't seem like enough. Should I try to find my benefactors so I could thank them and ask why they did it? That's when it hit me: I needed to accept the gift and pass it on.

Through Celebrate Recovery, God has given me a great second chance. I don't know why, because in my eyes I'm not worthy. But before I spend a lot of time and energy trying to figure out why, I think I'll accept the fact that Jesus thought I am worth the ultimate price! I can't wait to tell someone else God thinks they are worthy too.

Jesus said he came to "seek and save the lost." He also says we are his ambassadors, so our mission is his mission. Let's be on the lookout.

Lord God, thank you for your great act of kindness. I will tell everyone I see what you have done for me. In Jesus' name, Amen.

LUKE 20

*"The stone that the builders rejected
has become the cornerstone"*

LUKE 20 (ESV)

English Standard Version

THE AUTHORITY OF JESUS CHALLENGED

One day, as Jesus was teaching the people in the temple and preaching the gospel, the chief priests and the scribes with the elders came up

2 and said to him, "Tell us by what authority you do these things, or who it is that gave you this authority."

3 He answered them, "I also will ask you a question. Now tell me,

4 was the baptism of John from heaven or from man?"

5 And they discussed it with one another, saying, "If we say, 'From heaven,' he will say, 'Why did you not believe him?'

6 But if we say, 'From man,' all the people will stone us to death, for they are convinced that John was a prophet."

7 So they answered that they did not know where it came from.

8 And Jesus said to them, "Neither will I tell you by what authority I do these things."

THE PARABLE OF THE WICKED TENANTS

9 And he began to tell the people this parable: "A man planted a vineyard and let it out to tenants and went into another country for a long while.

10 When the time came, he sent a servant to the tenants, so that they would give him some of the fruit of the vineyard. But the tenants beat him and sent him away empty-handed.

11 And he sent another servant. But they also beat and treated him shamefully, and sent him away empty-handed.

12 And he sent yet a third. This one also they wounded and cast out.

13 Then the owner of the vineyard said, 'What shall I do? I will send my beloved son; perhaps they will respect him.'

14 But when the tenants saw him, they said to themselves, 'This is the heir. Let us kill him, so that the inheritance may be ours.'

15 And they threw him out of the vineyard and killed him. What then will the owner of the vineyard do to them?

16 He will come and destroy those tenants and give the vineyard to others." When they heard this, they said, "Surely not!"

17 But he looked directly at them and said, "What then is this that is written: " 'The stone that the builders rejected has become the cornerstone'?

18 Everyone who falls on that stone will be broken to pieces, and when it falls on anyone, it will crush him."

19 The scribes and the chief priests sought to lay hands on him at that very hour, for they perceived that he had told this parable against them, but they feared the people.

PAYING TAXES TO CAESAR

20 So they watched him and sent spies, who pretended to be sincere, that they might catch him in something he said, so as to deliver him up to the authority and jurisdiction of the governor.

21 So they asked him, "Teacher, we know that you speak and teach rightly, and show no partiality, but truly teach the way of God.

22 Is it lawful for us to give tribute to Caesar, or not?"

23 But he perceived their craftiness, and said to them,

24 "Show me a denarius. Whose likeness and inscription does it have?" They said, "Caesar's."

25 He said to them, "Then render to Caesar the things that are Caesar's, and to God the things that are God's."

26 And they were not able in the presence of the people to catch him in what he said, but marveling at his answer they became silent.

SADDUCEES ASK ABOUT THE RESURRECTION

27 There came to him some Sadducees, those who deny that there is a resurrection,

28 and they asked him a question, saying, "Teacher, Moses wrote for us that if a man's brother dies, having a wife but no children, the man must take the widow and raise up offspring for his brother.

29 Now there were seven brothers. The first took a wife, and died without children.

30 And the second

31 and the third took her, and likewise all seven left no children and died.

32 Afterward the woman also died.

33 In the resurrection, therefore, whose wife will the woman be? For the seven had her as wife."

34 And Jesus said to them, "The sons of this age marry and are given in marriage,

35 but those who are considered worthy to attain to that age and to the resurrection from the dead neither marry nor are given in marriage,

36 for they cannot die anymore, because they are equal to angels

and are sons of God, being sons of the resurrection.

37 But that the dead are raised, even Moses showed, in the passage about the bush, where he calls the Lord the God of Abraham and the God of Isaac and the God of Jacob.

38 Now he is not God of the dead, but of the living, for all live to him."

39 Then some of the scribes answered, "Teacher, you have spoken well."

40 For they no longer dared to ask him any question.

WHOSE SON IS THE CHRIST?

41 But he said to them, "How can they say that the Christ is David's son?

42 For David himself says in the Book of Psalms, " 'The Lord said to my Lord, "Sit at my right hand,

43 until I make your enemies your footstool." '

44 David thus calls him Lord, so how is he his son?"

BEWARE OF THE SCRIBES

45 And in the hearing of all the people he said to his disciples,

46 "Beware of the scribes, who like to walk around in long robes, and love greetings in the marketplaces and the best seats in the synagogues and the places of honor at feasts,

47 who devour widows' houses and for a pretense make long prayers. They will receive the greater condemnation."

△△△

C.U.B.E.

BIBLE STUDY METHOD

We used C.U.B.E. back in Luke 6 and Luke 13, so you probably know what's coming: it's time to Circle, Underline, Bracket, and Express.

(Circle)

Read Luke 20 again (out loud) but this time look for anything that has to do with God (Father, Son, or Holy Spirit). Put a (circle) around every mention of his name, including pronouns referring to him.

Underline

Read Luke 20 another time, but this time around, look for statements that talk about how a follower of Jesus *should live*. When you find such a statement, underline it.

[Bracket]

Read Luke 20 once more, but this time look for statements that talk about how a believer should *not* live. When you encounter such a statement, put a set of [brackets] around it.

Express

Congratulations! You have just read Luke 20 four times. Take a moment to express your worship and gratitude to God for anything he has revealed to you during your study.

RIDDLE ME THIS

DEVOTIONAL READING

*August 25 reading of John D. Barry and Rebecca Kruyswijk,
Connect the Testaments: A One-Year Daily Devotional with Bible
Reading Plan (Bellingham, WA: Lexham Press, 2012).*

"Now he is not God of the dead, but of the living,
for all live to him."" (Luke 20:38, ESV)

Jesus' enemies regularly attempted to make Him look foolish or to disprove His authority. The absurd questions they concocted to discredit Him are rather amusing. The Sadducees posed one of the most preposterous questions about the resurrection of the dead and its relevance to divorce (Luke 20:27–33): If a woman has been married seven times, whose wife will she be when the dead are resurrected?

This scene is especially humorous in light of rabbis' habit of playing mind games to outsmart (or "outwise") one another and the Sadducees' belief that resurrection does not exist. Jesus' opponents thought they had rigged the game: Any answer to their riddle would be incorrect. It was an attempt to trap Jesus into agreeing that the resurrection of the dead is a myth. Jesus, however, offered an answer that put them in their place (Luke 20:34–40). His response made the Sadducees look even more foolish in light of larger biblical theology about marriage and divorce.

More than 500 years before this conversation, Isaiah remarked, "Thus says Yahweh: 'Where is this divorce document of your mother's divorce, with which I dismissed her? or to whom of my creditors did I sell you? Look! you were sold because of your sin, and your mother was dismissed because of your transgressions' " (Isa 50:1). The Sadducees—along with the entire nation of Israel—had already been condemned for not honoring marriage in life.

So often we are concerned with logistics or details when our energy should be spent on discerning God's will for our lives and whether we are in that will. Like the Sadducees, we tell ourselves witty lies to get around doing the will of God. We somehow believe that if we can *reason* our way forward, we can justify our inactions. But as Jesus taught the Sadducees, in any game of riddles or reason, faith will always win.

What are you wrongly justifying or "witting" yourself out of doing?

ΔΔΔ

LUKE 21

"By your endurance, gain your lives"

LUKE 21 (CSB)

Christian Standard Bible

THE WIDOW'S GIFT

He looked up and saw the rich dropping their offerings into the temple treasury. He also saw a poor widow dropping in two tiny coins. "Truly I tell you," he said, "this poor widow has put in more than all of them. For all these people have put in gifts out of their surplus, but she out of her poverty has put in all she had to live on." As some were talking about the temple, how it was adorned with beautiful stones and gifts dedicated to God, he said, "These things that you see—the days will come when not one stone will be left on another that will not be thrown down."

"Teacher," they asked him, "so when will these things happen? And what will be the sign when these things are about to take place?"

Then he said, "Watch out that you are not deceived. For many will come in my name, saying, 'I am he,' and, 'The time is near.' Don't follow them. When you hear of wars and rebellions, don't be alarmed. Indeed, it is necessary that these things take place first, but the end won't come right away." Then he told them: "Nation will be raised up against nation, and kingdom against kingdom. There will be violent earthquakes, and famines and plagues in various places, and there will be terrifying sights and great signs from heaven. But before all these things, they will lay their hands on you and persecute you. They will hand you over to the synagogues and prisons, and you will be brought before kings and governors because of my name. This will give you an opportunity to bear witness. Therefore make up your minds not to prepare your defense ahead of time, for I will give you such words and a wisdom that none of your adversaries will be able to resist or contradict. You will even be betrayed by parents, brothers, relatives, and friends. They will kill some of you. You will be hated by everyone because of my name, but not a hair of your head will be lost. By your endurance, gain your lives."

"When you see Jerusalem surrounded by armies, then recognize that its desolation has come near. Then those in Judea must flee to the mountains. Those inside the city must leave it, and those who are in the country must not enter it, because these are days of vengeance to fulfill all the things that are written. Woe to pregnant women and nursing mothers in those days, for there will be great distress in the land and wrath against this people. They will be killed by the sword and be led captive into all the nations, and Jerusalem will be trampled by the Gentiles until the times of the Gentiles are fulfilled. Then there will be signs in the sun, moon, and stars; and there will be anguish on the earth among nations bewildered by the roaring of the sea and the waves. People will faint from fear and expectation of the things that are coming on the world, because the powers of the heavens will be shaken. Then they will see the Son of Man coming in a cloud with power and great glory. But when these things begin to take place, stand up and lift up your heads, because your redemption is near."

Then he told them a parable: "Look at the fig tree, and

all the trees. As soon as they put out leaves you can see for yourselves and recognize that summer is already near. In the same way, when you see these things happening, recognize that the kingdom of God is near. Truly I tell you, this generation will certainly not pass away until all things take place. Heaven and earth will pass away, but my words will never pass away.

"Be on your guard, so that your minds are not dulled from carousing, drunkenness, and worries of life, or that day will come on you unexpectedly like a trap. For it will come on all who live on the face of the whole earth. But be alert at all times, praying that you may have strength to escape all these things that are going to take place and to stand before the Son of Man."

During the day, he was teaching in the temple, but in the evening he would go out and spend the night on what is called the Mount of Olives. Then all the people would come early in the morning to hear him in the temple.

ΔΔΔ

MANUSCRIPT

BIBLE STUDY METHOD

The Manuscript Bible study method eliminates verse numbers and paragraph headings so we can focus on just the scripture itself.

In Luke 7 and Luke 14, we learned about the Manuscript Bible study method. So, you probably were not surprise to discover that Luke 21 didn't include any paragraph headings or verse numbers—as this is the distinguishing characteristic of a Manuscript Bible Study.

In a Manuscript study, you start with the basic text of the Bible with nothing else added—since chapter numbers, verse numbers, punctuation, and paragraph headings were actually added years later to our translations. What next?

Look For The W's:

Who is involved? *When* did it happen? *Where* is it happening? *What* is taking place? Ask yourself a few *why* questions regarding what Luke 21 is about.

Mark It Up!

Use a variety of colored pens and pencils to mark up the chapter. Don't worry about getting it "right," just mark it up.

Reflect, Pray, Act.

How does what you're reading and studying apply to you and where you are with God, others, etc.?

CALL BACK

DEVOTIONAL READING

December 19 reading of Lettie B. Cowman, Streams in the Desert (Los Angeles, CA: The Oriental Missionary Society, 1925), 362–363.

This will give you an opportunity to bear witness. (Luke 21:13, CSB)

L IFE is a steep climb, and it does the heart good to have somebody "call back" and cheerily beckon us on up the high hill. We are all climbers together, and we must help one another. This mountain climbing is serious business, but glorious. It takes strength and steady step to find the summits. The outlook widens with the altitude. If anyone among us has found anything worth while, we ought to "call back."

If you have gone a little way ahead of me, call back—
'Twill cheer my heart and help my feet along the stony track;
And if, perchance, Faith's light is dim, because the oil is low,
Your call will guide my lagging course as wearily I go.

Call back, and tell me that He went with you into the storm;

Call back, and say He kept you when the forest's roots were torn;
That, when the heavens thunder and the earthquake shook the hill,
He bore you up and held you where the very air was still.

Oh, friend, call back, and tell me for I cannot see your face;
They say it glows with triumph, and your feet bound in the race;
But there are mists between us and my spirit eyes are dim,
And I cannot see the glory, though I long for word of Him.

But if you'll say He heard you when your prayer was but a cry,
And if you'll say He saw you through the night's sin-darkened sky—
If you have gone a little way ahead, oh, friend, call back—
'Twill cheer my heart and help my feet along the stony track.

LUKE 22

"Do this in remembrance of me"

LUKE 22 (NLT)

New Living Translation

JUDAS AGREES TO BETRAY JESUS

The Festival of Unleavened Bread, which is also called Passover, was approaching.

2 The leading priests and teachers of religious law were plotting how to kill Jesus, but they were afraid of the people's reaction.

3 Then Satan entered into Judas Iscariot, who was one of the twelve disciples,

4 and he went to the leading priests and captains of the Temple guard to discuss the best way to betray Jesus to them.

5 They were delighted, and they promised to give him money.

6 So he agreed and began looking for an opportunity to betray Jesus so they could arrest him when the crowds weren't around.

THE LAST SUPPER

7 Now the Festival of Unleavened Bread arrived, when the Passover lamb is sacrificed.

8 Jesus sent Peter and John ahead and said, "Go and prepare the Passover meal, so we can eat it together."

9 "Where do you want us to prepare it?" they asked him.

10 He replied, "As soon as you enter Jerusalem, a man carrying a pitcher of water will meet you. Follow him. At the house he enters,

11 say to the owner, 'The Teacher asks: Where is the guest room where I can eat the Passover meal with my disciples?'

12 He will take you upstairs to a large room that is already set up. That is where you should prepare our meal."

13 They went off to the city and found everything just as Jesus had said, and they prepared the Passover meal there.

14 When the time came, Jesus and the apostles sat down together at the table.

15 Jesus said, "I have been very eager to eat this Passover meal with you before my suffering begins.

16 For I tell you now that I won't eat this meal again until its meaning is fulfilled in the Kingdom of God."

17 Then he took a cup of wine and gave thanks to God for it. Then he said, "Take this and share it among yourselves.

18 For I will not drink wine again until the Kingdom of God has come."

19 He took some bread and gave thanks to God for it. Then he broke it in pieces and gave it to the disciples, saying, "This is my body, which is given for you. Do this in remembrance of me."

20 After supper he took another cup of wine and said, "This cup is the new covenant between God and his people—an agreement confirmed with my blood, which is poured out as a sacrifice for you.

21 "But here at this table, sitting among us as a friend, is the man who will betray me.

22 For it has been determined that the Son of Man must die. But what sorrow awaits the one who betrays him."

23 The disciples began to ask each other which of them would ever do such a thing.

24 Then they began to argue among themselves about who would be the greatest among them.

25 Jesus told them, "In this world the kings and great men lord it over their people, yet they are called 'friends of the people.'

26 But among you it will be different. Those who are the greatest among you should take the lowest rank, and the leader should be like a servant.

27 Who is more important, the one who sits at the table or the one who serves? The one who sits at the table, of course. But not here! For I am among you as one who serves.

28 "You have stayed with me in my time of trial.

29 And just as my Father has granted me a Kingdom, I now grant you the right

30 to eat and drink at my table in my Kingdom. And you will sit on thrones, judging the twelve tribes of Israel.

JESUS PREDICTS PETER'S DENIAL

31 "Simon, Simon, Satan has asked to sift each of you like wheat.

32 But I have pleaded in prayer for you, Simon, that your faith should not fail. So when you have repented and turned to me again, strengthen your brothers."

33 Peter said, "Lord, I am ready to go to prison with you, and even to die with you."

34 But Jesus said, "Peter, let me tell you something. Before the rooster crows tomorrow morning, you will deny three times that you even know me."

35 Then Jesus asked them, "When I sent you out to preach the Good News and you did not have money, a traveler's bag, or an extra pair of sandals, did you need anything?" "No," they replied.

36 "But now," he said, "take your money and a traveler's bag. And if you don't have a sword, sell your cloak and buy one!

37 For the time has come for this prophecy about me to be fulfilled: 'He was counted among the rebels.' Yes, everything written about me by the prophets will come true."

38 "Look, Lord," they replied, "we have two swords among us." "That's enough," he said.

JESUS PRAYS ON THE MOUNT OF OLIVES

39 Then, accompanied by the disciples, Jesus left the upstairs room and went as usual to the Mount of Olives.

40 There he told them, "Pray that you will not give in to temptation."

41 He walked away, about a stone's throw, and knelt down and prayed,

42 "Father, if you are willing, please take this cup of suffering away from me. Yet I want your will to be done, not mine."

43 Then an angel from heaven appeared and strengthened him.

44 He prayed more fervently, and he was in such agony of spirit that his sweat fell to the ground like great drops of blood.

45 At last he stood up again and returned to the disciples, only to find them asleep, exhausted from grief.

46 "Why are you sleeping?" he asked them. "Get up and pray, so that you will not give in to temptation."

JESUS IS BETRAYED AND ARRESTED

47 But even as Jesus said this, a crowd approached, led by Judas, one of the twelve disciples. Judas walked over to Jesus to greet him with a kiss.

48 But Jesus said, "Judas, would you betray the Son of Man with a kiss?"

49 When the other disciples saw what was about to happen, they exclaimed, "Lord, should we fight? We brought the swords!"

50 And one of them struck at the high priest's slave, slashing off his right ear.

51 But Jesus said, "No more of this." And he touched the man's ear and healed him.

52 Then Jesus spoke to the leading priests, the captains of the Temple guard, and the elders who had come for him. "Am I some dangerous revolutionary," he asked, "that you come with swords and clubs to arrest me?

53 Why didn't you arrest me in the Temple? I was there every day. But this is your moment, the time when the power of darkness reigns."

PETER DENIES JESUS

54 So they arrested him and led him to the high priest's home. And Peter followed at a distance.

55 The guards lit a fire in the middle of the courtyard and sat around it, and Peter joined them there.

56 A servant girl noticed him in the firelight and began staring at him. Finally she said, "This man was one of Jesus' followers!"

57 But Peter denied it. "Woman," he said, "I don't even know him!"

58 After a while someone else looked at him and said, "You must be one of them!" "No, man, I'm not!" Peter retorted.

59 About an hour later someone else insisted, "This must be one of them, because he is a Galilean, too."

60 But Peter said, "Man, I don't know what you are talking about." And immediately, while he was still speaking, the rooster crowed.

61 At that moment the Lord turned and looked at Peter. Suddenly, the Lord's words flashed through Peter's mind: "Before the rooster crows tomorrow morning, you will deny three times that you even know me."

62 And Peter left the courtyard, weeping bitterly.

63 The guards in charge of Jesus began mocking and beating him.

64 They blindfolded him and said, "Prophesy to us! Who hit you that time?"

65 And they hurled all sorts of terrible insults at him.

JESUS BEFORE THE COUNCIL

66 At daybreak all the elders of the people assembled, including the leading priests and the teachers of religious law. Jesus was led before this high council,

67 and they said, "Tell us, are you the Messiah?" But he replied, "If I tell you, you won't believe me.

68 And if I ask you a question, you won't answer.

69 But from now on the Son of Man will be seated in the place of power at God's right hand."

70 They all shouted, "So, are you claiming to be the Son of God?" And he replied, "You say that I am."

71 "Why do we need other witnesses?" they said. "We ourselves heard him say it."

ΔΔΔ

YOU DECIDE

BIBLE STUDY METHOD

For the final three chapters of Luke, you get to decide what Bible Study Method to use. Pick one of the following methods to study, apply, and pray about Luke 22.

S.O.A.P.
R.E.A.P.
4R's
C.O.R.E
Discovery
C.U.B.E.
Manuscript

DO YOU CONTINUE TO GO WITH JESUS?

DEVOTIONAL READING

September 19 reading of Oswald Chambers, My Utmost for His Highest: Selections for the Year (Grand Rapids, MI: Oswald Chambers Publications; Marshall Pickering, 1986).

"You have stayed with me in my time of trial (temptations)." (Luke 22:28, NLT).

It is true that Jesus Christ is with us in our temptations, but are we going with Him in His temptations? Many of us cease to go with Jesus from the moment we have an experience of what He can do. Watch when God shifts your circumstances, and see whether you are going with Jesus, or siding with the world, the flesh and the devil. We wear His badge, but are we going with Him? "From that time many of His disciples went back and walked no more with Him." The temptations of Jesus continued throughout His earthly life, and they will continue throughout the life of the Son of God in us. Are we going with Jesus in the life we are living now?

We have the idea that we ought to shield ourselves from some of the things God brings round us. Never! God engineers circumstances, and whatever they may be like we have to see that we face them while abiding continually with Him in His temptations. They are *His* temptations, not temptations to us, but temptations to the life of the Son of God in us. The honour of Jesus Christ is at stake in your bodily life. Are you remaining loyal to the Son of God in the things which beset His life in you?

Do you continue to go with Jesus? The way lies through Gethsemane, through the city gate, outside the camp; the way lies alone, and the way lies until there is no trace of a footstep left, only the voice, *"Follow Me."*

∆∆∆

LUKE 23

"Father, forgive them"

LUKE 23 (NIRV)

New International Reader's Version

BEFORE PILATE

Then the whole group got up and led Jesus off to Pilate.
2 They began to bring charges against Jesus. They said, "We have found this man misleading our people. He is against paying taxes to Caesar. And he claims to be Christ, a king."

3 So Pilate asked Jesus, "Are you the king of the Jews?" "Yes. It is just as you say," Jesus replied.

4 Then Pilate spoke to the chief priests and the crowd. He announced, "I find no basis for a charge against this man."

5 But they kept it up. They said, "His teaching stirs up the people all over Judea. He started in Galilee and has come all the way here."

6 When Pilate heard this, he asked if the man was from Galilee.

7 He learned that Jesus was from Herod's area of authority. So Pilate sent Jesus to Herod. At that time Herod was also in Jerusalem.

8 When Herod saw Jesus, he was very pleased. He had been wanting to see Jesus for a long time. He had heard much about him. He hoped to see Jesus do a miracle.

9 Herod asked him many questions, but Jesus gave him no answer.

10 The chief priests and the teachers of the law were standing there. With loud shouts they brought charges against him.

11 Herod and his soldiers laughed at him and made fun of him. They dressed him in a beautiful robe. Then they sent him back to Pilate.

12 That day Herod and Pilate became friends. Before this time they had been enemies.

13 Pilate called together the chief priests, the rulers and the people.

14 He said to them, "You brought me this man. You said he was turning the people against the authorities. I have questioned him in front of you. I have found no basis for your charges against him.

15 Herod hasn't either. So he sent Jesus back to us. As you can see, Jesus has done nothing that is worthy of death.

16 So I will just have him whipped and let him go."

18 With one voice the crowd cried out, "Kill this man! Give Barabbas to us!"

19 Barabbas had been thrown into prison. He had taken part in a struggle in the city against the authorities. He had also committed murder.

20 Pilate wanted to let Jesus go. So he made an appeal to the crowd again.

21 But they kept shouting, "Crucify him! Crucify him!"

22 Pilate spoke to them for the third time. "Why?" he asked. "What wrong has this man done? I have found no reason to have him put to death. So I will just have him whipped and let him go."

23 But with loud shouts they kept calling for Jesus to be crucified. The people's shouts won out.

24 So Pilate decided to give them what they wanted.

25 He set free the man they asked for. The man had been thrown in prison for murder and for fighting against the authorities. Pilate gave Jesus over to them so they could carry out their plans.

JESUS IS NAILED TO A CROSS

26 As they led Jesus away, they took hold of Simon. Simon was from Cyrene. He was on his way in from the country. They put a wooden cross on his shoulders. Then they made him carry it behind Jesus.

27 A large number of people followed Jesus. Some were women whose hearts were filled with sorrow. They cried loudly because of him.

28 Jesus turned and said to them, "Daughters of Jerusalem, do not cry for me. Cry for yourselves and for your children.

29 The time will come when you will say, 'Blessed are the women who can't have children! Blessed are those who never gave birth or nursed babies!'

30 It is written, " 'The people will say to the mountains, "Fall on us!" They'll say to the hills, "Cover us!" '

31 People do these things when trees are green. So what will happen when trees are dry?"

32 Two other men were also led out with Jesus to be killed. Both of them had broken the law.

33 The soldiers brought them to the place called The Skull. There they nailed Jesus to the cross. He hung between the two criminals. One was on his right and one was on his left.

34 Jesus said, "Father, forgive them. They don't know what they are doing." The soldiers divided up his clothes by casting lots.

35 The people stood there watching. The rulers even made fun of Jesus. They said, "He saved others. Let him save himself if he is the Christ of God, the Chosen One."

36 The soldiers also came up and poked fun at him. They offered him wine vinegar.

37 They said, "If you are the king of the Jews, save yourself."

38 A written sign had been placed above him. It read, This Is the King of the Jews.

39 One of the criminals hanging there made fun of Jesus. He said, "Aren't you the Christ? Save yourself! Save us!"

40 But the other criminal scolded him. "Don't you have any respect for God?" he said. "Remember, you are under the same sentence of death.

41 We are being punished fairly. We are getting just what our actions call for. But this man hasn't done anything wrong."

42 Then he said, "Jesus, remember me when you come into your kingdom."

43 Jesus answered him, "What I'm about to tell you is true. Today you will be with me in paradise."

JESUS DIES

44 It was now about noon. The whole land was covered with darkness until three o'clock.

45 The sun had stopped shining. The temple curtain was torn in two.

46 Jesus called out in a loud voice, "Father, into your hands I commit my very life." After he said this, he took his last breath.

47 The Roman commander saw what had happened. He praised God and said, "Jesus was surely a man who did what was right."

48 The people had gathered to watch that sight. When they saw what happened, they beat their chests and went away.

49 But all those who knew Jesus stood not very far away,

watching those things. They included the women who had followed him from Galilee.

JESUS IS BURIED

50 A man named Joseph was a member of the Jewish Council. He was a good and honest man.

51 He had not agreed with what the leaders had decided and done. He was from Arimathea, a town in Judea. He was waiting for God's kingdom.

52 Joseph went to Pilate and asked for Jesus' body.

53 He took it down and wrapped it in linen cloth. Then he put it in a tomb cut in the rock. No one had ever been buried there.

54 It was Preparation Day. The Sabbath was about to begin.

55 The women who had come with Jesus from Galilee followed Joseph. They saw the tomb and how Jesus' body was placed in it.

56 Then they went home. There they prepared spices and perfumes. But they rested on the Sabbath day in order to obey the Law.

ΔΔΔ

YOU DECIDE

BIBLE STUDY METHOD

For the final three chapters of Luke, you get to decide what Bible Study Method to use. Pick one of the following methods to study, apply, and pray about Luke 23.

S.O.A.P.
R.E.A.P.
4R's
C.O.R.E
Discovery
C.U.B.E.
Manuscript

BLESSED REDEEMER

DEVOTIONAL READING

April 7 reading of Kenneth W. Osbeck, *Amazing Grace: 366 Inspiring Hymn Stories for Daily Devotions* (Grand Rapids, MI: Kregel Publications, 1996), 110.

"The soldiers brought them to the place called The Skull. There they nailed Jesus to the cross. He hung between the two criminals. One was on his right and one was on his left." (Luke 23:33, NiRV)

A Hill with Three Crosses—
One cross where a thief died IN SIN
One cross where a thief died TO SIN
A center cross where a Redeemer died FOR SIN
—Unknown

It is thought that the day we call "Good Friday" originated from the term "God's Friday"—the day that Christ was led to the hill of Golgotha and crucified, assuring an eternal reconciliation for lost man. The Roman cross, intended to be an instrument of cruel death, instead became an instrument of new life and hope for the human race. God loved and valued each of us so highly that He was willing to pay the greatest price imaginable for our salvation.

The composer of this hymn (Blessed Redeemer), Harry Dixon Loes, was a popular music teacher at the Moody Bible Institute from 1939 until his death in 1965. One day while listening to a sermon on the subject of Christ's atonement entitled "Blessed Redeemer," Mr. Loes was inspired to compose this tune. He then sent the melody with the suggested title to Mrs.

Christiansen, a friend for many years, asking her to write the text. The completed hymn first appeared in the hymnal *Songs of Redemption* in 1920.

Mrs. Avis Christiansen is to be ranked as one of the important gospel hymn writers of the 20th century. She has written hundreds of gospel hymn texts as well as several volumes of published poems. Throughout her long lifetime of 90 years, Mrs. Christiansen collaborated with many well-known gospel musicians to contribute several other choice hymns to our hymnals, including "Blessed Calvary" and "I Know I'll See Jesus Some Day."

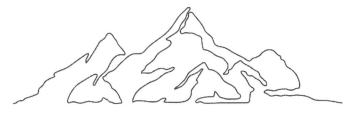

Up Calv'ry's mountain, one dreadful morn, walked Christ my Savior, weary and worn; facing for sinners death on the cross, that He might save them from endless loss.

"Father, forgive them!" thus did He pray, e'en while His life-blood flowed fast away; praying for sinners while in such woe—no one but Jesus ever loved so.

O how I love Him, Savior and Friend! How can my praises ever find end! Thru years unnumbered on heaven's shore, my tongue shall praise Him forevermore.

Chorus: Blessed Redeemer, precious Redeemer! Seems now I see Him on Calvary's tree, wounded and bleeding, for sinners pleading—blind and unheeding—dying for me!

Since Christ has paid the price of our redemption in full, all we have to do is believe, receive, rejoice and represent Him. Reflect on this musical truth—

ΔΔΔ

LUKE 24

"He is not here, but raised up"

LUKE 24 (MSG)

The Message

At the crack of dawn on Sunday, the women came to the tomb carrying the burial spices they had prepared. They found the entrance stone rolled back from the tomb, so they walked in. But once inside, they couldn't find the body of the Master Jesus. They were puzzled, wondering what to make of this. Then, out of nowhere it seemed, two men, light cascading over them, stood there. The women were awestruck and bowed down in worship. The men said, "Why are you looking for the Living One in a cemetery? He is not here, but raised up. Remember how he told you when you were still back in Galilee that he had to be handed over to sinners, be killed on a cross, and in three days rise up?" Then they remembered Jesus' words.

They left the tomb and broke the news of all this to the Eleven and the rest. Mary Magdalene, Joanna, Mary the mother of James, and the other women with them kept telling these things to the apostles, but the apostles didn't believe a word of it, thought they were making it all up. But Peter jumped to his feet and ran to the tomb. He stooped to look in and saw a few grave clothes, that's all. He walked away puzzled, shaking his head.

That same day two of them were walking to the village Emmaus, about seven miles out of Jerusalem. They were deep in conversation, going over all these things that had happened. In the middle of their talk and questions, Jesus came up and walked along with them. But they were not able to recognize who he was. He asked, "What's this you're discussing so intently as you walk along?"

They just stood there, long-faced, like they had lost their best friend. Then one of them, his name was Cleopas, said, "Are you the only one in Jerusalem who hasn't heard what's happened during the last few days?"

He said, "What has happened?"

They said, "The things that happened to Jesus the Nazarene. He was a man of God, a prophet, dynamic in work and word, blessed by both God and all the people. Then our high priests and leaders betrayed him, got him sentenced to death, and crucified him. And we had our hopes up that he was the One, the One about to deliver Israel. And it is now the third day since it happened. But now some of our women have completely confused us. Early this morning they were at the tomb and couldn't find his body. They came back with the story that they had seen a vision of angels who said he was alive. Some of our friends went off to the tomb to check and found it empty just as the women said, but they didn't see Jesus."

Then he said to them, "So thick-headed! So slow-hearted! Why can't you simply believe all that the prophets said? Don't you see that these things had to happen, that the Messiah had to suffer and only then enter into his glory?" Then he started at the beginning, with the Books of Moses, and went on through all the Prophets, pointing out everything in the Scriptures that referred to him.

They came to the edge of the village where they were headed. He acted as if he were going on but they pressed him: "Stay and have supper with us. It's nearly evening; the day is done." So he went in with them. And here is what happened: He sat down at the table with them. Taking the bread, he blessed and broke and gave it to them. At that moment, open-eyed, wide-eyed, they recognized him. And then he disappeared. Back and forth they talked. "Didn't we feel on fire as he conversed with us on the road, as he opened up the Scriptures for us?"

They didn't waste a minute. They were up and on their way back to Jerusalem. They found the Eleven and their friends gathered together, talking away: "It's really happened! The Master has been raised up—Simon saw him!" Then the two went over everything that happened on the road and how they recognized him when he broke the bread.

While they were saying all this, Jesus appeared to them and said, "Peace be with you." They thought they were seeing a ghost and were scared half to death. He continued with them, "Don't be upset, and don't let all these doubting questions take over. Look at my hands; look at my feet—it's really me. Touch me. Look me over from head to toe. A ghost doesn't have muscle and bone like this." As he said this, he showed them his hands and feet. They still couldn't believe what they were seeing. It was too much; it seemed too good to be true. He asked, "Do you have any food here?" They gave him a piece of leftover fish they had cooked. He took it and ate it right before their eyes. Then he said, "Everything I told you while I was with you comes to this: All the things written about me in the Law of Moses, in the Prophets, and in the Psalms have to be fulfilled."

He went on to open their understanding of the Word of God, showing them how to read their Bibles this way. He said, "You can see now how it is written that the Messiah suffers, rises from the dead on the third day, and then a total life-change through the forgiveness of sins is proclaimed in his name to all nations— starting from here, from Jerusalem! You're the first to hear and see it. You're the witnesses. What comes next is very important:

I am sending what my Father promised to you, so stay here in the city until he arrives, until you're equipped with power from on high." He then led them out of the city over to Bethany. Raising his hands he blessed them, and while blessing them, took his leave, being carried up to heaven. And they were on their knees, worshiping him. They returned to Jerusalem bursting with joy. They spent all their time in the Temple praising God. Yes.

ΔΔΔ

YOU DECIDE

BIBLE STUDY METHOD

For the final three chapters of Luke, you get to decide what Bible Study Method to use. The verse numbers and paragraph headings have been removed in case you'd like to use the Manuscript method.

S.O.A.P.
R.E.A.P.
4R's
C.O.R.E
Discovery
C.U.B.E.
Manuscript

EYES WIDE OPEN

DEVOTIONAL READING

January 24 and March 19 reading of Samuel G. Hardman and Dwight Lyman Moody, Thoughts for the Quiet Hour (Willow Grove, PA: Woodlawn Electronic Publishing, 1997).

...they were not able to recognize who he was...(Luke 24:16)

At that moment, open-eyed, wide-eyed, they recognized him. (Luke 24:31)

There is much precious significance in this. The Lord is often present in our lives in things that we do not dream possess any significance. We are asking God about something which needs His mighty working, and the very instrument by which He is to work is by our side, perhaps for weeks and months and years all unrecognized, until suddenly, some day it grows luminous and glorious with the very presence of the Lord, and becomes the mighty instrument of His victorious working. He loves to show His hand through the unexpected. Often he keeps us from seeing His way until just before He opens it, and then, immediately that it is unfolded, we find that He was walking by our side in the very thing, long before we even suspected its meaning. (A. B. Simpson)

"They came to the edge of the village where they were headed. He acted as if he were going on but they pressed him: 'Stay and have supper with us...'" (Luke 24:28,29)

Is not God always acting thus? He comes to us by His Holy Spirit as He did to these two disciples. He speaks to us through the preaching of the Gospel, through the Word of God, through the various means of grace and the providential circumstances of life; and having thus spoken, He makes as though He would go further. If the ear he opened to His voice and the heart to His Spirit, the prayer will then go up, "Lord, abide with me." But if that voice makes no impression, then He passes on, as He has done thousands of times, leaving the heart at each time harder than before, and the ear more closed to the Spirit's call. (F. Whitfield)

△△△

PASTOR PAUL'S RIBBON-TALLY METHOD

(FOR READING THE BIBLE)

T he Ribbon-Tally Method is a simple and flexible system I put together for reading through the entire Bible on a regular basis. I'd like to show you how to use this method in three simple steps.

1. Mark Each Section Of Your Bible With A Ribbon.

Of course, to complete this you'll first need to decide how many sections you'd like to divide your Bible into.

If you view your Bible as one big section, then the one bookmark your Bible likely came with will be enough; you could skip ahead to step two. But, I've personally discovered that I prefer to split my Bible up into multiple sections.

When I first started experimenting with this method, I split my Bible into 12 sections. That felt a bit ambitious, so then I went to 10 sections for a few years, but 10 sections also felt like a bit much. I've recently settled on *6 basic sections*, which is working well for me and the way I like to read my Bible. The sections I've chosen are:

Genesis — Deuteronomy
Joshua — Esther

Job — Song of Songs
Isaiah — Malachi
Matthew — Acts
Romans — Revelation

So, Let's say, like me, you choose to go with six sections. If that's the case, your bible is going to need 6 ribbons (which probably means you'll need to add additional ribbons). But, how do you do that?

Here's the easiest solution I've come up with. All you need is a generous length of satin 1/8" ribbon and some kind of durable tape—gaffer tape or duct tape are both good options.

Tear off a strip of tape that is a bit shorter than the length of your bible, and then cut 6 ribbon bookmarks that are about twice the length of your Bible. Now, take your ribbons and place them about halfway down the sticky side of the tape.

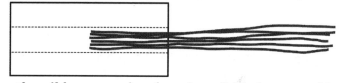

Once the ribbons are in place just fold the two sides of the tape over your ribbons, and then slip this completed multi-ribbon marker *into the spine* of your bible.

Now you just take each of your ribbon bookmarks and lay them at the beginning of the various sections of your bible.

One last thing you might want to do is cut the bookmarks to a length that looks nice and works for you. I think it looks nice to cut them at an angle, and I also like to burn the end of each ribbon to keep them from fraying.

2. Record Your Reading Start-Date On The First Page Of Each Section.

Find a place where you have plenty of place to write the date, because you're going to write the current date every time you begin reading each section.

I like recording the date because I enjoy seeing how long it took me to read any one section of the Bible—as well as how many times I've read it in the last year or so.

Let me also suggest a pen that I've found words for me. I use a *Pigma Micron 01 archival ink pen.* I like this pen the best because it doesn't bleed through the page and it also doesn't leave a blob of ink that a roller-ball pen can sometimes make. This pen is also great for making little notes right in your Bible.

3. Create A Tally Mark At The End Of Each Completed Passage.

By passage, I usually mean chapter. But occasionally, I'll split up a long chapter into a few passages. The best example of that is Psalm 119 where I've put tally marks after every two to three sections of this Psalm.

WHY USE THE RIBBON-TALLY METHOD?

You might be wondering *why* I developed the Ribbon-Tally Method. Here's four advantages I've discovered while using it.

1. It's Simple.

All you truly need is a Bible, a pen, and a few ribbons. That's it.

2. It's Flexible.

How so? Well, You can read in any order you want. Sometimes I start with the last bookmark. Sometimes I start with the first bookmark. Sometimes I start somewhere in the middle. I find that changing up the order helps to keep things fresh.

You can also spend as much time in any section as you want. Let's say you intend to read six passages of Scripture. If that's the case, you could read one passage from each section, or you could choose to read six passages from one section, or two passages each in three different sections. It's completely up to you.

3. It's Encouraging.

As the years go by, your Bible serves as a record of the number of times that you have read any particular passage, and how long it's taken you to complete any one section.

4. It's Distraction-Free

The Ribbon-Tally Method uses a physical, hard copy, battery-free version of the Bible. This means there are no notifications or pop-ups that a digital Bible might have. It's just you, your Bible, a pen, and the Holy Spirit.

If you decide to use *Pastor Paul's Ribbon-Tally Method* for Reading the Bible, please let me know how it goes. I'd also love to hear about anything you've done to modify the method to make it work best for you.

ACKNOWLEDGEMENT

I think it's important to emphasize that I (Paul) didn't really *write* this book. It's more like I compiled and edited it. Sure, there's a few of my thoughts sprinkled here and there, but I'd wager that 99% of *Seize the Word and Hold on No Matter What* is: 1) Bible passsages (which are obviously not written by me), 2) Bible study methods developed mostly by *others,* and 3) devotional passages that are written by a variety of past and present authors.

That said, I would still like to express apprecation to a few people.

To Patty, for always believing in my little side projects (which seem to crop up when we are already busy with other projects). You give me space and time to do what I feel led to do, and that has always been so meaningful to me. I also deeply admire your daily commitment to reading through the Bible.

To my dad, this book wouldn't be in your hands if not for your incessant pestering through text messages and phone calls to encourage me to get working on my next book! I've still got more in me, so keep up with the pestering. I don't mind. Also, your devotion to memorizing the Word inspires me. 500 verses and counting! Amazing!

To Professor Grant Horner. You don't know me, but the Bible reading plan named after you (Professor Grant Horner's Bible-

Reading System) was inspiration for my Ribbon-Tally method I make mention of in this book. I appreciate your devotion to devouring the Word of God.

To you, the reader! If you enjoyed <u>Seize the Word and Hold on No Matter What,</u> one of the best ways you can thank me is to post a review on Amazon, Goodreads, or another online platform. Thank you!

ABOUT THE AUTHOR

Paul Durbin

Before answering the call from God to move to Boulder, Colorado, Paul led a large, vibrant international church in Beijing, China.

Every week, several thousand people from 70+ nations and a wide variety of Christian church backgrounds would gather for worship.

Despite the many inherent differences in such a diverse group —under Paul's leadership—this congregation enjoyed a unified culture of palpable unity and love. A common comment from visitor's was, "this must be what Heaven feels like."

Paul currently lives in Boulder Colorado where he and his wife Patty have founded Belay Church. If you joined one of their gatherings in Boulder, you'd notice Paul and Patty's knack for gathering a diverse group. They often have several cultures and nations represented under their roof—people from Asia, Africa, Europe, the America's, etc. A guest at a recent event was overheard to say, "In all my years in Boulder, I've never been around such a diverse group!"

This gift for fostering an environment of unity has a direct influence on the creation of Seize the Word and Hold on No Matter What. Rather than pitting one Bible translation or study method against another, Paul shows how there is great value in engaging several of each.

Married since 1993, Paul and Patty have four amazing kids who love one another, and love Jesus.

Paul has been engaged in full-time Christian ministry since 1991—serving in a variety of roles: youth pastor, worship leader, police chaplain, college ministry, church leadership, ministry network leadership, and overseas ministry.

Paul can be reached at www.pauldurbin.co.

BOOKS BY THIS AUTHOR

When Jesus Stole My Bread

We're created to live at the intersection of Grace and Truth, yet we often gravitate toward one or the other. "When Jesus Stole My Bread" uses the power of parable—a fictionalized story of the young boy who surrendered his loaves and fish to Jesus—to help us live at the convergence of life-transforming Truth and Spirit-empowered Grace.

Four Things In Your Heart

Your heart has four valves, and four chambers. But did you know it has four other things as well? Eternity is one of them...which could be forever changed by reading this book.

Nextstop

While there are hundreds of subway stops scattered around Beijing, four stops must take priority: Know God, Be Family, Go Deep, Make Impact. You won't find these stops on a subway line, of course. You will discover them as you commit to a journey of connecting with God's plan for your life. That is the purpose of this book—to provide daily inspiration for these life-changing stops. Where are you on this journey? What is your nextstop?

Made in United States
Troutdale, OR
09/02/2025

34186174R00164